P9-CEB-024

THE GLORIOUS SCOUNDREL

OTHER BOOKS BY NOEL B. GERSON

Fiction

Nonfiction

THE GLORIOUS SCOUNDREL

A BIOGRAPHY OF
CAPTAIN JOHN SMITH

by Noel B. Gerson

DODD, MEAD & COMPANY, NEW YORK

1. 2. 3. 4 5 6 7 8 9 10

Library of Congress Cataloging in Publication Data

Gerson, Noel Bertram, date
  The glorious scoundrel.

  Bibliography: p.
  Includes index.
    1. Smith, John, 1580–1631. 2. Explorers—
Great Britain—Biography. 3. Jamestown, Va.—History.
I. Title.
F229.S7G47   973.2′1′0924 [B]   78–1357
ISBN 0–396–07518–5

For Anne Wendy Brennan

THE PORTRAICTUER OF CAPTAINE IOHN SMITH ADMIRALL OF NEW ENGLAND.

These are the Lines that shew thy Face; but those
That shew thy Grace and Glory, brighter bee:
Thy Faire-Discoueries and Fowle-Overthrowes
Of Salvages, much Civillizd by thee
Best shew thy Spirit; and to it Glory Wyn;
So, thou art Brasse without, but Golde within.

Self-portrait of Captain John Smith, from his map of New England

Above: Whale hunting off Newfoundland, from Plancius' map "Nova Francia," 1592–94

Left: Pocahontas saving the life of John Smith, from T. de Bry, *America*, Part XIII, 1634

Left: An Indian town of Powhatan's confederacy, from T. de Bry, *America*, Part I, 1590

The only known portrait of Pocahontas, *below*. She was twenty-one when the portrait was painted in 1616. *Smithsonian Institution.*

Ætatis suæ 21. Aᵒ. 1616.

Matoaks als Rebecka daughter to the mighty Prince Powhatan Emperour of Attanoughkomouck als Virginia converted and baptized in the Christian faith, and Wife to the Wor.ᵗ Mʳ Tho. Rolff.

Smith's map
of Virginia

Insert from Smith's map of Virginia showing Powhatan crowned with feathers

Heir manner of feeding is in this wife. They lay a matt made of bents one the grownde and fett their meate on the mids therof, and then fit downe Rownde, the men vppon one fide, and the woemen on the other. Their meate is Mayz fodden, in fuche forte as I defcribed yt in the former treatife of verye good tafte, deers flefche, or of fome other beafte, and fifhe. They are verye fober in their eatinge, and trinkinge, and confequentlye verye longe liued becaufe they doe opprefs nature.

Drawing of southeast Indians eating typical food, from T. de Bry, *America*, Part I, 1590

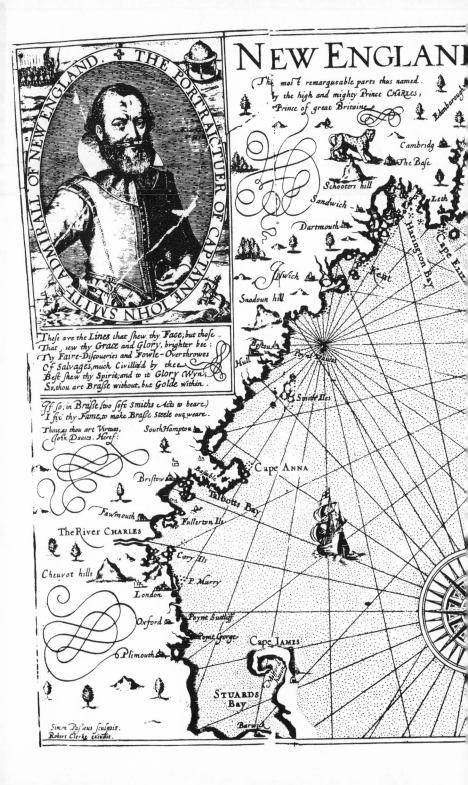

NEW ENGLAND

The most remarqueable parts thus named.
by the high and mighty Prince CHARLES,
Prince of great Britaine.

THE PORTRAICTVRE OF CAPTAINE IOHN SMITH ADMIRALL OF NEW ENGLAND.

These are the Lines that shew thy Face; but those
That shew thy Grace and Glory, brighter bee:
Thy Faire-Discoueries and Fowle-Overthrowes
Of Salvages, much Civilliz'd by thee
Best shew thy Spirit; and to it Glory Wyn;
So, thou art Brasse without, but Golde within.

If so; in Brasse (too soft smiths Acts to beare)
I fix thy Fame, to make Brasse Steele out weare.
Thine as thou art Virtues,
John Dauies. Heref:

Edenborough
Cambridg
The Base
Schooters hill
Sandwich
Dartmouth
Leth
Cape Eliz
Harrington Bay
Kent
JWich
Snadoun hill
Reston
Point Dauies
Hull
Smithe Iles
SouthHampton
Bristow
Bassable
Cape ANNA
Talbotts Bay
Fawmouth
Fullerton Ils
The River CHARLES
Cary Ils
Cheuyot hills
P. Murry
London
Oxford
Poynt Sutliff
Pont Gorge
Cape IAMES
6 Plimouth
STUARDS Bay
Milford hauen
Barwick

Simon Passæus sculpsit.
Robert Clerke excudit.

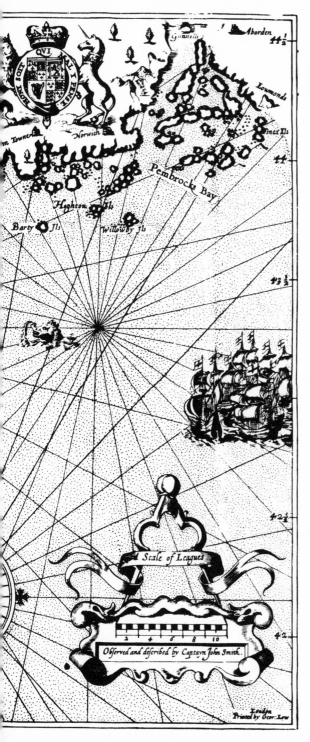

Smith's map
of New England

1

THE paradox of Captain John Smith is that he had no need to embellish and embroider his truly great achievements to attain the fame after which he thirsted. A burning desire for recognition characterized many great explorers of the age—such as Cabot, Raleigh, and Henry Hudson—but John Smith outdid them all in his yearning for glory. It is ironic that his ceaseless attempts to thrust himself into the limelight clouded the true value of his exploits.

John Smith was a remarkable man of many talents: an explorer, cartographer, administrator, soldier, and author of distinction. He wrote eight books about his adventures, and those on his explorations in the New World were long regarded as authoritative. It is thanks to John Smith's remarkably accurate map of 1614 that what was then considered the northern part of Virginia is now known as New England. Cape Cod, too, owes its name to Smith. He also made marvelous maps of Chesapeake Bay and Virginia.

It is unfortunate that one of the most romantic legends in American history may be just that: a legend, and one which casts a distorting shadow over the figure of a great man who was also a great scoundrel. Possibly little Poca-

1

hontas did save the life of the English adventurer, but it is more probable that Smith never met the daughter of the Chickahominy sachem until she visited the court of King James as Mrs. John Rolfe. Smith's attempt to cash in on the sensation she made during her brief visit to England in 1616–1617 obscured his more important deeds, including the true story of his dealings with Pocahontas's father, the powerful Powhatan. As a consequence the names of John Smith and Pocahontas have become permanently intertwined.

Such contradictions were typical of Smith's life. He preferred the title of Captain, a rank he won outside the service of his own king, to President of Virginia or Grand Admiral of New England and the Fishing Banks. These grander titles would have caused less skepticism among his contemporaries, who found it difficult to believe that one man could be both a ship's captain and the head of a military company, as Smith variously referred to himself. Although these claims were true, when combined with Smith's glowing accounts of his own exploits they were difficult for the ordinary Englishman to accept.

He was a tireless propagandist of the New World, and he spent the better part of his life trying to persuade his countrymen to settle that vast wilderness. He had proved through his own efforts at Jamestown that permanent colonization was possible. He knew that the real wealth of the new continent lay not in gold and diamonds, but in its vast resources of timber, furs, and fish. Nevertheless, the more he contributed to the effort of colonization, the less he received in return. An unscrupulous adventurer, he allowed himself to be cheated by the colonizing companies.

2

He gave the Separatist leaders of the Plymouth experiment the information they needed to survive. He planned to sail on the *Mayflower*, but his flamboyant personality did not fit in with the somber Separatists, and his habit of assuming absolute command alienated the leaders of the Pilgrims, who hired Captain Miles Standish in his place. Although the colonization of New England had been John Smith's greatest dream, he refused to admit the success of the Plymouth colony, simply because he had been rejected as its military leader.

Richard Hakluyt, the greatest geographer of the age, who may have taught Smith the fundamentals of cartography, recognized the worth of Smith's accomplishments, as did Henry, Prince of Wales. Had Henry lived to succeed his father, James I, Smith's achievements would have been recognized by the Crown. And had Hakluyt lived, Smith might have won the academic acceptance he craved. Anyone with an interest in the New World owned copies of John Smith's books, yet he was never officially recognized by the academicians of Oxford and Cambridge.

Hakluyt was buried in Westminster Abbey. Sir Walter Raleigh, to whom Smith had blatantly advertised his loyalty during Raleigh's imprisonment, was executed, making him a martyr. Henry Hudson, a recipient of much of Smith's information, was abandoned by his crew on that great body of water that now bears his name; this misfortune assured his immortality. John Smith, however, was unlucky even in death.

He died in bed in his cheap living quarters, circumstances so uninspiring that the event passed unnoticed. Only a handful of friends attended his funeral in the church of St. Sepulchre. Even this modest tomb was temporary: the church was destroyed in the Great Fire of London thirty-five years later.

The royalties from his books were awarded to the Crown after Smith's brother and sister fought a bitter court battle, each claiming to be the sole beneficiary of his will. But England was fighting its Civil War, and an ironic fate directed that the money end in the hands of Oliver Cromwell, to be used by the sober Puritans. Even Smith's books were losing their popularity as other New World settlers published their own accounts of conditions there.

Perhaps Smith would have been amused had he known that one of his most enduring monuments in popular thought is the legend he invented, the tale of the little Indian princess who risked her life to save a strange warrior.

2

GEORGE and Alice Smith were tenant farmers of Lord Willoughby de Eresby, of Lincolnshire, but they were different from the other tenant farmers of the area. George Smith was a member of the gentry, with a coat of arms passed down through at least five generations, and with several parcels of pasturelands and orchards of his own. The Smiths were frequently invited to the Willoughby manor, a mark of importance in a status-conscious society.

John Smith was born on January 2, 1579. Seven days later Lord Willoughby acted as his godfather at the baptism.

John's mother, Alice, was a great influence on his life. Blonde, fair-skinned, and lovely, she was worshiped by her husband and two sons. John tried for his whole adult life to find a woman who could measure up to his memories of her.

By the time he was four years old John had been assigned chores on the farm, and by six or seven he was being sent to the grammar school at Alford, a few miles to the north. There he learned English, Latin, Greek, and arithmetic, and in the old tradition of English schools he was caned for incorrect answers.

It was an exciting time to be alive, a time of expanding frontiers, not only geographical but intellectual. John, with his close friend and classmate, Lord Willoughby's second son, spent hours reading and studying in the Willoughby library. This was the golden age of Elizabeth I, the time of Francis Bacon and William Shakespeare, and the boys were caught up in the intellectual ferment.

When John was nine years old he and the younger Willoughby boy were sent to a more demanding school, the grammar school at Louth. All the other pupils were sons of nobles, and perhaps for the first time John Smith was forced to fight for social acceptance.

In that same year Philip II of Spain, worried by England's growing nationalism and power under Queen Elizabeth, sent his huge armada of ships against the island nation. The courage of the English defense created an enduring legend. Severely beaten by the English, the remnants of the armada were then scattered by a great storm. The English were wild with rejoicing, and the exploits of Sir Francis Drake made their mark on the impressionable nine-year-old, John Smith.

In that same summer he and the Willoughby boys decided to build themselves a boat, in reality a crude raft, and set out on the treacherous North Sea. John was master of the craft, which was fortunately rescued by a returning fishing boat. In Smith's later account of the incident he mentions, quite casually, that neither he nor his nobly born "crew" could swim.

The great deeds of England's adventurer-heroes continued to fire John's imagination, such exploits as those of the admirals Raleigh, Howard, and Essex, who sailed into the harbor of Cádiz and successfully sank or burned the fifty galleons of a newly forming Spanish armada.

When John was sixteen his formal education came to an end, since only those young men of means with a real passion for learning went on to university. John wanted to apply for a commission in the new Royal Navy that Queen Elizabeth had established. His parents realized that he had no training for such a career, however, and apprenticed him to Thomas Sendall, a great merchant. John subsequently went off to the town of Lynn, where Sendall had his business. His parents had reason to feel that his future was assured.

Whatever John thought his apprenticeship would entail—perhaps acting as one of Sendall's agents abroad—he quickly discovered he was required to sit all day, writing letters and keeping the books. John might have considered running away, but his father's death in 1596 left him with seven acres of pastureland, three orchards, and livestock. John's younger brother, Francis, received rent-producing houses in Louth; his sister, Alice, was willed only personal mementos and a little cash.

John's luck came in because Lord Willoughby had been named the executor of the estate. He was able to sell the livestock to Willoughby, putting half of the cash aside for himself and giving the other half to his mother. He then persuaded both Lord Willoughby and Sendall to let him go to Orléans, France, where the elder Willoughby boy had just completed his education. John's father would probably have denied him permission, but Lord Willoughby was sending his younger son in any case, and was easily persuaded to let John go, too. He even gave John an extra ten pounds from his inheritance.

The two boys went to London, spending a fascinated week there instead of sailing directly for Boulogne as they had promised. London was still a provincial city compared to Paris, Madrid, or Rome, but to two country boys it was a magnificent wonder. There were theaters and taverns everywhere, and most of the streets were cobbled. They found the mounds of garbage in the street to be no hindrance.

For the first and last time in his life, John drank to excess. The experience was an unfortunate one; apparently allergic to alcohol, he broke out in a painful rash and became very ill. Eventually he recovered, of course, but never again did he overindulge.

The other delights of London were less harmful to him. He tried his luck at gaming, and discovered he had the instincts of a born gambler. But his risks after that time were taken with his life, his own fortune, and the vast fortunes of others in undertakings considerably more daring than a roll of dice. John also found female companionship, and discovered that he was almost irresistibly attracted to women.

John was loath to leave the city but was finally persuaded by the younger Willoughby, who was anxious to meet his brother. Accordingly they took passage on a small Channel boat, which unaccountably dropped them at St. Valery-sur-Somme instead of at Boulogne. Because they were already late for their arranged meeting with Thomas Willoughby, the boys resisted temptation and detoured around Paris. When they arrived at Orléans they discovered that Thomas, tired of waiting for them, had gone off to Paris himself. They were delighted to follow.

Paris was the cosmopolitan city that London was not, and its impact on the young John Smith was enormous. The city teemed with visitors from all over Europe, there were more inns and theaters than in London, and there were large private parks within the city's limits, some stocked with game and protected by guards. The architecture was magnificent, the art treasures of the cathedrals dazzling, and marble statues were even displayed in the open.

John enjoyed himself greatly, spending time with Sir Thomas Willoughby's friends. One of those he met was a young Scotsman, one David Hume. Hume was short of cash, but led John to believe that he had powerful friends at the court in Edinburgh. John gave Hume most of his own funds in return for letters of introduction to the young Scot's "friends" at court, who would presumably obtain for John a commission in the Royal Highland Guards. Hume stressed the need for secrecy, and John, young and gullible, went along with the plan.

Needless to say, Hume's friends were fictitious, as Henry Willoughby pointed out when John finally revealed the plan on their homeward journey. Even had Hume's connections been real, they would have been of no help to John. King James, son of Mary, Queen of Scots, would eventually succeed Elizabeth, his mother's executioner. Nevertheless, he lived in such fear of assassination by the English that he would admit no Englishman to his court, much less to his personal guard.

John's plans were in ruins. His purse was almost empty, and if he went back to Lynn to resume his apprenticeship with Sendall he knew he could not obtain another leave of absence. By the time he reached journeyman's status with Sendall he would be too settled to seek adventure.

John's solution to his problem was as drastic as it was startling. He told Henry Willoughby that he intended to enlist in the French army as a volunteer. Unable to dissuade John, Henry was forced to return home alone, carrying letters to John's mother, Sendall, and Lord Willoughby. He asked his mother and Lord Willoughby for understanding, but curtly informed Sendall that he was not cut out for the life of a merchant.

3

H<small>AD</small> John Smith bothered to ask, almost anyone could have told him his idea was foolish. The army of King Henry IV, a brilliant ruler, was an elite corps of professional soldiers. There was no opening in the ranks of these trained and tried men for an amateur. Smith had no skills, and even worse he knew only a few words of French.

When he reached headquarters of the French army, near Le Havre, he was turned away by a recruiting sergeant. His refusal to leave, and his coolness in the face of aggressive teasing by the amused soldiers caught the attention of an English-speaking French captain, who suggested that Smith try one of the mercenary companies at the far end of the bivouac. Mercenary soldiers were considered scoundrels, but Smith's purse was empty, and he had no intention of returning to England. In effect, he had no choice.

Captain Joseph Duxbury, thirty-year-old youngest son of a baron, and a renegade Englishman, was always glad to welcome a fellow countryman to his rough company. Duxbury had been forced to flee England to escape debtors' prison and now had to his name a suit of silver armor he had stripped from a corpse on the battlefield, a large number of weapons, and a magnificent stallion. His company, which numbered one hundred men at full strength, was composed of men like himself.

In order to join this select band Smith allegedly had to fight their champion, one Luis de Toledo, a professional killer who did not know the meaning of fair play. Smith, who believed in the English ideal of sportsmanship, was knocked senseless, but nonetheless fought well enough to be admitted to the company. The experience was a lesson in the ways of the world, where victory is not always achieved by adherence to principle. Smith learned his lesson well.

Smith's uniform was a steel helmet, which he was issued; his weapon was a harquebus, an incredibly unreliable musket almost as dangerous to the man who fired it as to the enemy. Food was provided each morning, but the mercenaries had not been paid in months, and there was no sign that this situation would change. Smith had no horse and no blanket and no warm clothes, and no means of attaining these things short of taking them from a dead foe. Unfortunately there was no sign of any foes, alive or dead, for many weeks.

These first weeks were miserable. He slept in a coarse tent without a blanket, and, having no funds, had nothing to do during the day while his companions gambled and drank. One night his pistol vanished, and when he discovered it the next day in the possession of another mercenary, the man calmly denied it. Thereafter Smith strapped his sword to his leg at night.

Smith was able to find temporary relief from his boredom in the village of Harfleur, where he wandered one day. A local butcher needed an assistant, and Smith, although no expert, knew enough of the trade from his boyhood on a farm to qualify. The young man who had spurned a position as a wealthy merchant's apprentice leaped at the chance to earn a tiny amount of pay and a hearty dinner served every night by the butcher's wife.

The other soldiers did not have Smith's knack for keeping out of trouble, and the peace of Le Havre was constantly broken by drunken brawls. Unfortunately for Le Havre, the war was at a standstill while King Henry consolidated his gains; the Vatican no longer opposed him and had ceased its secret financial support of his enemies. Henry had not only forgiven many nobles who had opposed him, but had given some of them important positions in his government.

One of these men was Charles, Duc de Mayenne, who had nominal command of the army in the north. Mayenne was paying a visit to the governor of Le Havre when the bored French troops and their equally bored mercenary allies disrupted the town with their vicious quarrels.

Henry, Duc de Montmorency, the King's deputy, made a personal investigaton of the case. He was a superb military leader, and the commanders of the units involved remained loyal to him although their men had not been paid wages in months. Knowing the negotiations with Philip of Spain would fail and that he would need every man when the war resumed, Montmorency was reluctant to jeopardize their loyalty. He decided to let Mayenne, whom he disliked and distrusted, take the blame for the situation.

He suggested that Mayenne send the mercenaries ahead to the Amiens region to seek out and defeat a Spanish force there. Le Havre would have a respite, and Philip would be taught a lesson. Montmorency refrained from mentioning that the mercenaries would find the tracking of elusive Spanish cavalry unpopular, and that Mayenne would be blamed. Mayenne fell for the scheme and decided to take personal charge of the expedition.

The troops marched fruitlessly for eleven days, which did nothing to improve their dispositions. Food was rationed meagerly, but Mayenne, who weighed well over three hundred pounds, always had the best of everything.

On the twelfth day accident changed their luck. The Spaniards had camped near the small town of Grandvilliers, near Amiens, and their commanders were being entertained by the town's lord, Sieur Guy de Beauchamp, a former subordinate of Mayenne, when Mayenne had fought against Henry. De Beauchamp, however, had not changed sides.

The Spaniards were warned of the mercenaries' approach and fled into the walled town, accompanied by de Beauchamp and his family. Mayenne ordered his mercenaries to lay siege to Grandvilliers, but Captain Duxbury had his own priorities.

Duxbury led his company to the abandoned de Beauchamp manor, which they immediately sacked. John Smith did not accompany them in this exercise; he made straight for the stables where he acquired a horse, two saddles, a thick wool cloak, and an old double-edged sword. In an incredibly short time he had promoted himself from infantry to cavalry. He also availed himself of the opportunity to get rid of the hated harquebus, considering the sword a convenient substitute. He then tested his ability to bargain, and ended up with a pair of boots and a poniard in exchange for one of the saddles.

Duxbury's company was the most successful in this

"clash" with the enemy, the others gaining nothing. De Beauchamp had managed to convince Mayenne that the Spanish commander was merely paying a courtesy visit. Under the rules of chivalry, which had not yet been discarded, the Spaniards were allowed to leave and the siege was called off. In return the Spanish promised to leave immediately for the Belgian plains. When the commanding officers signed the agreement that night, only Duxbury's company was able to fully celebrate, with the provisions looted from the manor house.

There was a continuing need to guard the loot, for other mercenary companies were jealous of Duxbury's good fortune and wanted to help themselves to a share of it. There was a further complication when de Beauchamp demanded that his valuables be returned to him. Mayenne conveyed this order to Duxbury, who refused, knowing his men would not stand for it. Mayenne eventually gave in, and the Sieur de Beauchamp was forced to recover many of his valuable goods from a Le Havre pawnbroker with whom Duxbury's men did business. The proceeds were divided, with Smith receiving one share, a not inconsiderable sum. He was now a full-fledged professional soldier.

4

THE first test of John Smith's skill as
a fighting man came at the siege of Amiens in 1597, when
the Spanish broke the truce and captured the town.
Henry IV himself took command of his army, with
Montmorency as his second-in-command. The professional troops were under the command of Charles, Duc
de Biron, a talented but unstable general.

De Biron assigned the mercenaries one of the most
difficult tasks: patrolling the heavy woods on the north
and east sides of Amiens to make sure no supplies got
through to help the besieged. The terrain was treacherous, the work was exhausting, and the mercenaries were
frequently harassed by snipers from the walls, or by
unexpected sorties of the Spanish cavalry. But they were
paid regularly, and food was plentiful; Henry understood the needs of his soldiers.

John Smith took part in many of these actions, but he
makes only one outstanding claim. According to his own
report in *The True Travels, Adventures and Observations of
Captain John Smith,* he and three of his fellows were patrolling a section between the city wall and some deep
woods when they relaxed their vigilance and were ambushed by a platoon of Spaniards in armor, on

16

horseback. The four mercenaries were caught in a trap between a dangerous gully and the charging enemy.

Smith supposedly saved the day. He stopped his companions from fleeing and rode directly toward the Spaniards, at full gallop. He badly wounded the enemy officer, but the rest of the platoon continued its charge. Smith then threw aside his musket, snatched his pistol, and with his first shot brought down a horse in the front rank. By this time his friends had rallied and, under Smith's directions, presumably sent the enemy into a swift retreat back to the city. If this story is true it must indeed have been a highlight, for sieges were generally known for their tedium.

The siege did give Smith the opportunity to meet King Henry, who rode out daily to see his troops and frequently shared night patrol with them. Smith was greatly impressed by him, claiming in *True Travels* that but for Henry's influence he would have returned to his farm in England, ending his adventurous career.

The siege dragged on through spring and into the hot summer. The Spanish sent an enormous supply train under the guard of four regiments to try to relieve the city. They managed to draw Biron's troops out of position, and made a successful dash through the gates. Duxbury's company recovered in time to retaliate, inflicting damage on the Spanish rear guard. John Smith, surprisingly, gives no details of this engagement in the *True Travels*, although he was promoted to sergeant as a direct result.

Henry summoned more troops and by the end of August was able to completely seal off Amiens. The city surrendered on September 25, just as a messenger from Philip of Spain arrived to negotiate for peace. The war

17

between France and Spain was at an end, and Amiens could not be looted because it was a French town. Biron paid off the soldiers; the disappointed mercenaries, including nineteen-year-old Sergeant John Smith, had to look elsewhere for employment.

The obvious place to go was Amsterdam, as Philip of Spain was still trying to subdue the Dutch. The hereditary Stadtholder of Holland and Zeeland, the President of the Dutch Council of State, was Maurice of Nassau, a peace-loving young man interested in the arts and in overseas exploration. But he was forced to temporarily abandon his peaceful pursuits in 1598, for France was making peace with Spain, England was not pursuing the war, and he was left on his own. On his own, the peace-loving Maurice proved himself a military genius.

With thirteen Dutch regiments and six mercenary cavalry companies Maurice held off the great armies of Spain. His military intelligence agents were excellent, and Maurice was able to outmaneuver his enemies, frequently occupying terrain where they intended to launch surprise attacks before they could get there. Because of his generalship the Spanish made no gains on Dutch soil.

When Philip of Spain unexpectedly died the Dutch gained breathing space. But the house of Hapsburg, the rulers of Spain and Austria, took the opportunity to devise a cynical scheme requiring the Archduke Albert, Cardinal-Bishop of Vienna, to leave the Church and marry the Infanta Isabella, his cousin and Philip's daughter. They would then rule the Netherlands as a presumably new and independent nation.

Pope Clement VIII, a sincere man and a practical statesman, would neither release Albert from his vows nor sanction the marriage if Albert left the Church in any case. Nor would Maurice and the Dutch stand idly by. The situation continued to be excellent for the employment of mercenaries. Duxbury's company took part in several assaults against the Spanish in 1599.

After Albert and Isabella were married, despite the Pope, Maurice went on the offensive. On July 1, 1600, the Dutch attacked Albert at the town of Nieuport on the English Channel. The siege could have lasted indefinitely, as the town could be reinforced from the sea, but Maurice lured the Spanish garrison into the open by sending a ridiculously small force against the town.

When Albert sent his regiments into the open the mercenaries charged, placing themselves between the Spanish and the town. The Dutch troops followed, and Albert was forced to send his remaining units out as reinforcements. John Smith fought so brilliantly in this ferocious assault against the Spanish that he was mentioned in Maurice's report to the States-General: "The paid horsemen rode in the van, and were inspired by the example of an English sergeant in the Duxbury company, one Jon Smyt [sic], who laid about him with such rapid strokes that he left a path of Spanish dead in his wake."

Maurice won a spectacular victory, but the results for John Smith were less fortunate. Although he won fame from his mention in Maurice's report, he was seriously injured by a pistol fired at close range. Duxbury took charge of his horse and equipment while Smith was left behind in the home of De Groet, a Nieuport merchant, to recuperate.

Smith spent six months recovering, long after the Dutch had marched back to Amsterdam in triumph. His stay in the De Groet household was abruptly terminated when the merchant found Smith entertaining his daughter in the middle of the night. When Smith arrived back at Duxbury's company, hungry and tired, he found that Duxbury had promoted him to ensign, which made him third in command of the company. John Smith was an officer.

When it was reported that the Spanish were taking the field again before going into winter quarters, Maurice marched to meet them in Flanders, where Smith had his first experience with an independent command in brief skirmishes. But Albert did not intend to repeat his mistakes, and did not allow himself to be overwhelmed. When snow fell in November he made peace overtures to Maurice, and the frugal States-General, over the protests of Maurice, discharged the mercenaries. Maurice remembered Smith and gave him six double gulden in parting, a sum worth well over four thousand dollars today.

Most of Duxbury's company decided to enlist under the Hapsburgs to fight the Turks, but Smith had had enough of fighting for a while. He spent some time in Amsterdam with Duxbury, who had not gone with his company, and it was there that he met Peter Plancius, one of the greatest geographers of the age.

Plancius was the associate and counterpart of England's Richard Hakluyt, a man so enthralled by the exploration of the unknown parts of the earth that he sometimes forgot to eat for days. A strange friendship sprang up between the scholar and the ruthless young soldier, and Smith spent many days with Plancius, listening to the geographer and studying his charts. When he left he was fired with a dream of new continents, and he carried with him an introduction to Hakluyt.

Smith found passage home on an English merchant ship en route from the Mediterranean. Her master was one Henry Hudson, who had sailed with Captain John Davys on a voyage of discovery to the New World. Smith struck up an immediate friendship with him, and by the time they reached London they had thoroughly discussed Plancius's theories. Smith spent a week at Hudson's home in London, where Hudson expounded his theory of an unobstructed water passage across the North American continent to the East Indies. They maintained their friendship until Hudson's tragic death in pursuit of this obsession.

Also during that week Smith presented Plancius's letter to Hakluyt, Archdeacon at Westminster. Smith is uncharacteristically modest in his reports, even in the *True Travels*, of his association with Hakluyt. He was obviously deeply influenced by the great scholar, but he does not mention the fact that he must have made a very favorable impression in return. It was from this friendship that the Virginia colony eventually grew, as well as Smith's great voyage of discovery to New England.

Finally, in that winter of 1600, Smith rode north to Lincolnshire, laden with gifts for his family and with a magnificent new wardrobe for himself. His purse was filled with money, he was an officer, and at twenty-two years of age he felt himself to be a great success, deserving of a warm welcome.

5

JOHN SMITH returned home in time to celebrate Christmas with his mother, whom he found unchanged. But little else had remained the same. His brother was married to a girl of whom he disapproved, and his sister, Alice, was sufficiently grown to resent interference in her life, particularly in regard to suitors. Henry Willoughby, Smith's boyhood friend, was in London hoping to be appointed to a diplomatic post, and the elder brother had succeeded to his father's title.

Smith soon became bored with his placid existence, for he had very little in common with anyone around him. Perhaps his boredom and his recent brush with men of great learning inspired him to embark on his next experience, one completely out of character with the course of his life to that point.

He built himself a cabin deep in the forests of the Willoughby estate and retired there for six months, living primarily on the game he shot. He came out once a week to visit his mother, but spent most of his time reading, borrowing many of his books from the Willoughby library. In his book *The True Travels*, Smith specifically mentions studying Hakluyt's works on the New World. He also became familiar with *The World*, a collection of maps Plancius had published. By the summer of 1601 he had achieved the equivalent of a higher education and was once again ready for adventure.

Adventure was not as easy to find as Smith had hoped. No British troops were overseas, as King James was cautiously refusing to openly provoke his Spanish enemy. Privateers, however, were tacitly encouraged to attack Spanish merchant ships, provided the Treasury received eight shillings for every pound captured. Smith decided against this course of action, preferring to offer his services as a Christian mercenary against the Turks in central Europe.

His relatives wanted him to invest in farmland but he was adamant. In July 1601 he said goodbye to his mother; he never saw her again. He gave his money to his brother Francis to hold against his return, and traveled to London. There he visited Hakluyt, Hudson, and Henry Willoughby before sailing for France late in July.

John Smith's account of his experiences in his *True Travels* is nothing short of incredible. His fantastic adventures, told with no substantiation other than his own word, were a chief cause of the doubt that shadowed his reputation in his own time and thereafter. All the shipwrecks, mutinies, piracy, and hair-raising exploits that he claimed could not possibly have happened to one man, no matter how daring, in the space of six months.

Some of his accounts may have been true, however. He did spend several months on a Breton privateer in the Mediterranean, and his phrasing of the episode indicates that the Bretons were pirates and that he was more than a guest, becoming actively involved with them. In any event, in this interlude he was able to acquire a consider-

23

able sum with which to augment his meager funds. In the winter of 1602 he landed at Naples and traveled north to Rome.

Once in Rome he visited Jesuit headquarters, where he debated theology with some of the most learned men of the Roman Catholic Church. For many years this story was considered just another of Smith's fabrications, but in 1792 records were discovered in the archives of the Society of Jesus confirming that "an English gentleman, John Smyth," was indeed a guest there in 1602.

When Smith resumed his journey he took great care to avoid Venice, a fact that lends weight to the theory the Breton privateer attacked one or more Venetian merchantmen in the Mediterranean. The rulers of Venice kept lists of such wrongdoers, torturing and executing any they captured. It is possible that only such a significant deterrent would have been sufficient to keep John Smith from one of the wealthiest and most sophisticated cities on the Continent.

By the time he reached Vienna he had found no one enlisting mercenaries. He was told to seek out the Archduke Ferdinand, who was directing military operations in Graz, the provincial capital of southern Austria. He proceeded to Graz, where he found the army, and also a peculiar political situation.

Rudolph, Holy Roman Emperor of the German states, and a rival of the Hapsburgs of Austria, was lending only half-hearted cooperation in their common war against the Turks. Rudolph, an incredible bigot even for the seventeenth century, had dismissed all his Protestant officers, including Hungarian noblemen who had fought for more than twenty years under the imperial banner.

24

Ferdinand of Austria lost no time in enlisting these men in his own forces.

Smith did not completely understand the situation. Fearing that Ferdinand, too, might be accepting only Catholics, he presented his letter of recommendation from the Jesuits. This maneuver brought him to the attention of the Earl of Volda-Meldritch, who later became Smith's superior and his good friend, whom Smith referred to as Meldri.

Meldritch was one of the Hungarian Protestants taken into Ferdinand's service, and now he and his artillery commander, Baron Kizel, were forming a corps of their own. He was a deceptively mild and unassuming man who took a fierce enjoyment in battle.

The Earl was intrigued by Smith's cunning in presenting his letter from the Jesuits, interviewed him, and then hired him as a lieutenant on his personal staff. A multilingual aide would be of great value in a corps with men of many nationalities. Smith marched with Meldritch's unit to the scene of the fighting, Transylvania, now a part of Rumania. There they joined the overall command of Prince Sigismund Bathory, who had lost his wife and son to the enemy ten years previously.

The Turks came from a culture completely unlike any that John Smith had yet encountered. They were extremely sophisticated, reading the Koran, enjoying poetry and music, and living in silken tents. They also subjected captives to horrible torture, were magnificent fighting men, and were fanatically courageous. One of their most formidable fighting units was the Janissary Corps, made up entirely of former Christian slaves. These slaves were captured enemy soldiers who had been subjected to harsh training conditions and complex psychological stresses that resulted in their complete conversion to their captors' cause.

Encounters in this war were frequent and violent. No quarter was given on either side, a situation indicating the end of the "age of chivalry" and the beginning of modern warfare. Smith, naturally, claimed a dramatic part in one of these skirmishes.

When the cavalry detachment with which he was riding was ambushed, Smith engaged in hand-to-hand combat with a Turkish officer. The curved blade of his opponent was much more effective than his own sword, and Smith managed to wrest it from him after only narrowly avoiding decapitation. The officer fought on with foolhardy courage, brandishing a short knife, and Smith was forced to kill him to disengage. When the Turks withdrew they left their own dead behind. Smith rapidly realized that they were fighting a ruthless enemy.

At this time Sigismund was besieging the garrison of a Turkish-held town near the Hungarian-Transylvanian border, called Alba Regalis by everyone but the Germans, who called it Stühlweissenburg. Meldritch's unit was sent up to the siege lines almost as soon as it arrived. Here Smith first met the Janissaries in combat, when they rode out from the walls in forays.

Smith was fascinated by Greek fire, and he credits himself with a refinement of the "wet" fire, produced by burning substances such as sulphur and pitch, which give off an intense heat and are difficult to extinguish. His idea was that gunpowder and bullets should be added to the caldrons, and the whole covered with heavy canvas. When these caldrons were catapulted over the enemy walls, the damage would be doubled. The Greek

26

fire would do its usual work, and exploding bullets would fly in every direction.

Fifty such caldrons were secretly prepared, then catapulted into the heaviest concentrations of Turkish troops. This was done at midnight while the enemy slept, and the resulting carnage was ferocious. The infantry followed this barrage by storming the town, and before dawn the garrison surrendered.

The Turkish commander gave his sword to Meldritch, who in turn handed it to Smith. Along with the sword went a promotion to Captain, a title Smith was to use for the rest of his life. He was also given command of a mixed company of cavalry and light infantry, two hundred men in all. He was responsible directly, and only, to Meldritch.

Smith took his new responsibilities seriously, giving the welfare of his men first consideration. Because his company was composed of men of several nationalities and languages, he devised a signal system to communicate his orders in battle. The morale of his company was an example to others, and John Smith became a familiar figure to everyone in the army.

6

ORASTIE, a Transylvanian farm town, had once been a glamorous and busy city, but it had changed hands so often in the sixteenth and seventeenth centuries that it had lost its influence as a trade center. Sigismund had to capture Orastie if he wished to go farther into Transylvania, but he was reluctant to risk many of his men, as he knew there were strong Turkish reinforcements to the south. There was a large Christian population in the city, making an artillery assault out of the question. The Earl of Meldritch also wished the city spared for personal reasons: he had been born there. These factors combined to make investment of the town an extremely difficult problem.

The commander of the Turkish defense had his problems, too. As a younger brother of the Sultan Mohammed, Suleiman was afraid he would be executed if he lost too many men or had to summon help from another jealous brother, who would send bad reports of him to Constantinople. Suleiman knew that the war placed a great burden on the resources of the throne.

So for several weeks the two forces faced each other across the ramparts, shouting insults over the walls. Tempers understandably grew shorter and shorter. Finally a courier rode out of Orastie carrying a peculiar message: a challenge to personal combat, issued by a very bored Turkish noble. Turbashaw, as this gentleman was called, offered to meet any Christian in the army, armed with only a lance and a sword, although both duelists were to be mounted. The messenger also carried a letter from Suleiman to Sigismund, suggesting that a truce be declared for the purpose. John Smith was the most insistent of the would-be Christian champions, and Sigismund reluctantly agreed.

In a scene reminiscent of the great days of chivalry, the two armies took up positions outside the city walls while salutes and greetings were exchanged. Turbashaw appeared with considerable pomp, surrounded by slaves, but Smith presumably made his appearance unattended. Naturally the Turk did not have a chance, or so Smith wrote in his *Travels*. Smith killed his opponent with the first thrust of his lance. He claimed neither his enemy's horse nor his armor, but decapitated him and took the head back to Sigismund.

The Turks, of course, were not pleased. Another of their officers challenged Smith, with the object of regaining his comrade's head. Smith was not to be dissuaded, even by his friend the Earl of Meldritch, and rode out into the field to accept the challenge.

The scene was repeated the next day with similar pageantry, although Smith wore his usual unadorned armor. In this combat pistols were permitted, as well as swords and lances. Smith was forced to use his, after his first attempt to unseat his opponent failed. Although the man was merely injured he was momentarily incapacitated, and Smith took the opportunity to decapitate him. This time he did claim his enemy's horse and armor. The siege was resumed within the hour.

The Western high command knew of Suleiman's reluctance to ask for reinforcements and hoped to starve his army into submission, thus avoiding violence to the Christian population. The strategy was effective, and the Turks made several desperate but unsuccessful attempts to get supplies into Orastie. Sigismund and his generals were afraid another attempt might succeed.

While the officers debated what to do, Smith came forward with his own idea. He wanted to issue his own challenge to personal combat, convinced that the Turkish officers would not be able to pass up this chance for revenge. Suleiman, it was hoped, would make no attempt to send for supplies or help until the duel had been fought. The Earl of Meldritch opposed the idea, fearing the loss of a valuable officer, but Sigismund thought the life of only one mercenary was worth the gamble. The challenge was sent and accepted.

Then the plays for time began. Smith's seconds claimed he was ill, and forty-eight hours passed before negotiations could be resumed. For another four days, during which the siege still held, messengers were sent back and forth discussing the weapons to be used. At last the decision was made: pistols, scimitars, and battle-axes. John Smith, unfortunately, had no experience at all with the battle-ax and had to undergo a twenty-four-hour crash-course in its use.

The Turkish champion was an officer by the name of Buenimolgri, to whom Smith refers in *True Travels* as Bonny Mulgro. He was a colonel of heavy cavalry, an expert in the use of weapons. Smith's friends were not cheerful when they learned the news.

The Turks made their usual grandiose display, and Smith noted that Bonny Mulgro was a giant. But Smith made no display and showed no fear. When the signal was given, they charged each other full tilt.

Both men missed with their unreliable seventeenth-century firearms, then continued the combat with battle-axes. A duel of this sort required strength, courage, and skill, for the combatants needed both hands to wield the heavy, razor-sharp weapons. The mounted duelists were forced to guide their horses with their knees.

Although Smith was unaccustomed to using a battle-ax, for a while he gave as good as he received. Eventually, however, he slipped in his stirrups. When the Turk pressed forward, overconfident, to finish him off, Smith found an opening for his scimitar. Bonny Mulgro was dead, and Smith decapitated him.

For a few minutes it seemed as if a battle might erupt before the gates of Orastie, as the enraged Turks tried to ride Smith down. But both commanders and their generals managed to restore order, and the Turks marched back into the city. The siege resumed.

Smith enjoyed his personal triumph. His companions formed a procession in his honor, and the Earl of Meldritch congratulated him. Sigismund was even more appreciative. He gave Smith a stallion from his own stable, a gem-studded scimitar, and the sum of three hundred silver ducats, worth well over six thousand dollars. As Smith had no desire to carry so much money around camp with him, he left it in the safekeeping of the Prince's treasurer. This later proved to have been an extremely wise decision.

Suleiman made two final attempts to send messages for help, but both couriers were captured. Suleiman surrendered unconditionally, and Orastie was captured without violence to the inhabitants.

7

In the weeks that followed Smith went ahead with Meldritch's corps, which acted as a vanguard to scout out enemy territory. When necessary they cleared the region of small forces of Turks that might harass the main army when it advanced. Smith's battalion led the corps and fought in several skirmishes. The Earl of Meldritch was able to penetrate deep into enemy territory.

Communications were unfortunately poor, and Meldritch failed to realize that he was greatly outdistancing Sigismund's main army, which was weighed down with heavy siege equipment. The Turks' intelligence was good, however. They were aware of Meldritch's increasing isolation, and they wanted a victory.

Crimean Tatar troops, descendants of the Mongol hordes that centuries earlier had invaded Finland and Hungary, now formed crack Turkish regiments. Living in Lithuania and Poland, they had retained many of their ancient ways, although they had adopted Islam. They were magnificent horsemen and preferred death to defeat. Six thousand of these men were sent north, along with two regiments of Janissaries and three of Turkish dragoons, to annihilate Meldritch's force.

The Turks watched Meldritch as he crossed the rugged Transylvanian Alps. When he reached the narrow valleys of the Oltu River, a branch of the Danube, he was a full ten-day march ahead of Sigismund. The Turks waited in a wooded valley with towering hills on both sides and a steep climb ahead. They stationed archers and musketeers on these high points and sent the infantry around the Christians' rear to cut off retreat. Meldritch recognized the trap too late.

Smith's vanguard was ordered to hold the enemy while the rest of the force tried to erect a barricade of stakes made from pine trees to slow the enemy charge. Smith was able to hold off the Turks until the makeshift palisade was complete. He and his battalion then pulled back to safety. Meldritch's hope was to hold off the Turks until nightfall, then escape to the north over the rugged, heavily wooded terrain.

The Turks charged, exerting pressure from all sides, although the stakes slowed them slightly. Meldritch's cavalry was useless within the palisade, and casualties were heavy. The Christians were not able to take the offensive, only trying to beat off the enemy assault—until they ran out of ammunition. By late afternoon the Turks advanced without serious opposition.

Meldritch managed to escape capture by hiding in the brush, having been convinced by his officers of the terrible fate that would await him at the Sultan's hands. The officers themselves were not so lucky. Some tried to swim the river to the safety of higher ground, but were drowned by the weight of their armor. Most of the corps were killed, and a relatively few survivors were taken prisoner. John Smith was one of these.

His status as an officer was indicated by his silver

armor, a fact that probably saved his life. When he was found unconscious on the battlefield, he was spared and taken into the Turkish camp. In the morning he found himself with about fifty other officers, stripped naked and guarded by Janissaries.

Smith assumed that he, too, would be forcibly enlisted in the Janissaries. He did not know that for the past two years Constantinople's policy had changed, and no more prisoners were being taken for that purpose. The captives were marched south through the Alps, almost naked in the bitter winter weather, chained together. The overseers, however, took care to see that no one died; the prisoners were too valuable for that.

Eventually they reached Tchernavoda, a large town on the Danube at the southern border of Transylvania, winter headquarters for the Turkish army in Europe. There the prisoners were cleaned, fed, and treated by physicians. They were then taken to the slave market to be sold.

Smith was purchased by a pasha named Timor for three gold pieces, a large sum. He was taken in chains through Macedonia and Thrace to the city of Adrianople, about thirty miles from Constantinople. There he was fascinated by the blend of cultures: minarets and churches, Greek buildings and ancient Roman structures. Of the very few women who appeared on the narrow streets, all without exception were heavily veiled; but Smith had learned better than to indicate too great an interest in the ladies.

He was taken to the palace of Eski Serai, formerly a royal residence, where Timor now had a suite. The great palace was incredibly beautiful, with arched door frames, tiled floors, and lovely geometric designs. Smith lived in fear, with no idea of what was to become of him. His identity had become known, however, and Timor was pleased to own the winner of the celebrated duels. In fact, the pasha fabricated a story of having defeated Smith in combat, thus enhancing his own reputation.

Smith remained for several weeks in Adrianople. He insists, in *True Travels*, that Timor had him dressed in feminine attire; perhaps the pasha considered this a joke on the English champion. Eventually Smith was moved under guard to his final destination, the great city of Constantinople, once known as Byzantium.

Formerly a great Christian city, Constantinople had been, since its fall in 1453, the capital of the Ottoman Empire. Its beautiful harbor was filled with ships, and the minarets of the mosques towered above the walls of palaces. Aqueducts built in the fourth century by Constantine the Great, the city's founder, still brought water down from the hills, and games were still held every week in the ancient hippodrome.

Smith was delivered to a substantial red stone house, far removed from the ghetto quarters where many of the poor lived in ramshackle huts. The house belonged to Lady Charatza Tragabigzanda, a Turkish noblewoman betrothed to Timor. A portrait of her, sketched by Smith in later years, shows her with fair skin, delicate features, and reddish hair, possibly colored by henna. Smith was presented to her as a gift from Timor.

Tragabigzanda was pleased with the gift, and apparently decided to relieve some of the monotony of her existence as a typical Turkish noblewoman, forbidden even to appear in public unless heavily veiled and escorted, by having Smith perform the duties of a serving-maid. He was once again attired as a woman, in an all-feminine household. Smith considered himself fortunate, however, in that he was not forced to join Tragabigzanda's staff of eunuchs.

Smith had one friend during this troubling time, a young woman, also English and a slave, by the name of Elizabeth Rondee. Although they had little opportunity in the strictly supervised household to exchange confidences, Smith wrote in *True Travels* that she was the daughter of a British diplomat serving in Portugal. The vessel on which she and her parents were returning to England was attacked by Moslem pirates. Elizabeth saw both her parents killed, and she herself was sold into slavery, eventually ending up in the house of Tragabigzanda.

Tragabigzanda must have realized the budding friendship and natural sympathy between the two English slaves. Although European slaves were status symbols, Tragabigzanda avoided possible trouble in her household by separating them, sending Elizabeth to a cousin in a distant province. Smith was now completely alone, with no means of escape.

He was not the type, however, to remain satisfied with simple survival, and he sought definite means to improve his condition. He discovered that Tragabigzanda had a limited knowledge of Italian, a language with which he was also slightly familiar. Using this as a base, he began to teach her French, which he knew well. It was not long before they were able to communicate.

When Smith told her the true story of his capture in the Transylvanian Alps, Tragabigzanda's contempt for him changed to sympathy. She ceased treating him as a servingmaid and began to consider him as a friend. In Tragabigzanda's world, however, a woman's friendship with any man not her husband or brother was suspect, if not grounds for the death penalty. Tragabigzanda's relation with Smith, her servants suspected, went beyond friendship.

Rumors of the affair eventually came to the attention of the noblewoman's mother, who was understandably alarmed. Although Tragabigzanda's father was dead, Timor might well learn the truth. Tragabigzanda was eventually persuaded that the best protection consisted of sending Smith away from Constantinople. They would be safest, she thought, if he joined Timor in Cambia.

Smith agreed with her reasoning and even made the journey by himself, without a guard, traveling by ship and passing as a free man. That he made no attempt to escape indicates his possible regard for Tragabigzanda and his reluctance to cause her any embarrassment.

Timor had nothing to gain by treating Smith as gently as Tragabigzanda had. An iron collar was riveted around his neck and he lived in miserable slave pens, mistreated even by the other slaves, to whom he was a newcomer. During the day he labored hard in the fields. Smith spent more than a year under these conditions.

One day in February 1604 Smith unexpectedly found himself alone, working as a thresher in a barn. He took advantage of the situation and threw himself onto a pile of hay to rest. Unfortunately, Timor came by on an inspection tour, found him sleeping, and began to beat him viciously with a riding crop. Unable to stand any more, Smith picked up his heavy threshing bat and beat out Timor's brains.

Rather belatedly, Smith realized what he had done. He had no choice now but to try to escape, and he stripped

Timor's body and dressed in the pasha's clothes. He also took Timor's weapons: a pistol, scimitar, and short knife. He was even lucky enough to find Timor's horse outside the barn, and remembered to stuff his pockets with the rye he had been threshing. Unhesitatingly he rode to the northeast, toward Russia, the only nearby Christian nation, although one almost completely unknown to Westerners.

He managed to avoid army patrols and other travelers, stealing food from farms along his way. For sixteen days he continued northward, traveling mostly at night. He made his way through Turkish-dominated Transylvania and Moldavia, and avoided all inhabitants with such success that he later estimated that he had crossed the border and spent forty-eight hours in Russia without even realizing it.

8

O_{NCE} Smith crossed over the border, his situation did not immediately improve. Foreigners in Russia have always been regarded with, at best, intense suspicion, and the seventeenth century was no exception. Peasants and travelers alike fled the disreputable-looking Smith, and he was turned away from the gates of the walled towns. Only when he reached Rostov did he find help.

Rostov was a seaport located on the River Don, just a few miles from the Sea of Azov, the extension of the Black Sea. The capital of a grain-producing district, it had been occupied in the past by Mongols and Turks but had retained its typically Russian character. Tsar Boris Godunov maintained a strong garrison there; he had seized the throne by dubious methods, and he felt the need of upholding a position of strength.

Rostov was perhaps the strangest city of all those Smith had visited. It was a city of many churches, but they resembled none of the churches Smith had seen anywhere else in his travels. In fact, they were closer to Turkish mosques than to Christian houses of worship, although they had some of the characteristics of Greek temples. Not until later did he learn that the Russian church did not accept the authority of the Roman Pope.

As was usual for the time, the contrast between the magnificent homes of the wealthy and the misery of the poor was apparent, but it was even greater here than it had been in Constantinople. The nobles lived in castles that bordered both sides of the River Don. Smith was quick to note that each was capable of self-defense.

Smith had his first view of Rostov under guard. He was taken into custody at the city's walls by the Governor's grim-looking soldiers. None of them spoke any of the languages Smith knew, and their fierce behavior led him to believe that he might be killed immediately. Instead they took him to the Governor, Baron Reshdinski, an astounding man.

Reshdinski was both cultivated and contradictory. He spoke Greek, Turkish, and Latin as well as Russian, and was a student of French poetry. He loved music and fine food, and collected magnificent portraits painted on porcelain (after his death these went to the Kremlin in Moscow, to be preserved for posterity). He had some less savory habits, however: he would frequently "entertain" his dinner guests by having a serf tortured during the course of the meal, and the attractive peasant women of the neighborhood were terrified of him, as he was said to have fathered at least forty children without the consent of the mothers.

Reshdinski was immediately responsive to the cultivated young Englishman, and listened sympathetically to his story. Smith's slave collar was removed, his beard and hair were trimmed, and he enjoyed his first bath in months. Smith was one of the very few outsiders ever to come to Rostov, and the Governor was fascinated by him. Smith stayed at the castle as a guest, eating huge

Russian meals and wearing fur-trimmed suits.

Smith was both intrigued and horrified by Russian customs. When he went hunting with Reshdinski he was appalled by the nobles' habit of using serfs, instead of dogs, to flush their game. If the game, such as a wild boar, were cornered and turned on its attackers, serfs instead of dogs were often killed, but the Governor and his nobles were unmoved. Yet these same aristocrats often wept at a minstrel's romantic ballad.

More important to Smith than his friendship with Reshdinski was his relationship with the Governor's niece, Lady Camallata. Porcelain portraits of her still exist in the Kremlin, revealing her as a delicate blonde beauty. She was also learned and witty, speaking several languages, and she became Smith's natural and almost constant companion. During his three months in Rostov she managed to teach him Russian. Smith claims in his *True Travels* that he lost his heart to her.

In the spring of 1604 Camallata made a trip to Moscow and Smith went with her, traveling with a trade caravan, which used camels as well as horses and donkeys as pack animals. As Camallata was the Governor's niece, they traveled with an escort of Cossack cavalrymen. These soldiers were the descendants of nobles who had traditionally formed the bodyguards of the tsars, and Smith was impressed with their horsemanship, which he mentions in *True Travels*.

Moscow was a dismal city of wooden houses set in the midst of an enormous pine forest on the banks of the Moskva River. The only impressive buildings were the structures of the Kremlin Palace, an enormous fortress where Tsar Boris Godunov lived. Most of the nobility in the dingy capital had apartments there, too. Divisions of infantry and cavalry were stationed within the walls.

Beyond the Kremlin were two ornate cathedrals and another walled enclave, the Kitai Gorod. It was here that the city's merchants lived and worked. There were no other important buildings except for the Vasili Cathedral, begun during the reign of Ivan the Terrible and still incomplete.

Smith had no chance to explore what little there was to be seen in the city. When he attempted to venture from his own small suite in the Kremlin to inspect the city, he was halted at the gates by heavily armed Cossacks. He was informed that foreigners were not permitted to roam at will in the capital. This Russian attitude of suspicion greatly annoyed Smith, who made no friends among the nobles in the Kremlin. Most, in fact, went out of their way to avoid him.

Smith was shrewd enough to realize that politics, at least in part, lay behind the coldness of the Muscovites. The Tsar, although competent, had little personal following and was regarded in many quarters as an upstart. Rumors of plots and dissident armies forming in Poland and elsewhere kept the tension at a high level. No one wanted to give the Tsar the least cause for suspicion.

Smith met no high officials of the Russian government. He spent much of his time with Camallata, who had few official duties. He was not surprised, however, when he eventually received a firm invitation to leave the country, the only reason being that he was a foreigner.

Smith seems to have truly loved Camallata. He indicates in *True Travels* that he asked her to marry him and return with him to England. Camallata, however, was a true Russian, with a true Russian's love for her homeland. However she felt about Smith, she refused to leave her native land for him. Smith never forgot her, and he dedicated the first edition of his first book, *A True Relation,* to her.

Smith left Moscow without Camallata, provided with clothes and a horse by Baron Reshdinski, and escorted by Cossacks. The Cossacks left him at the Dneister River, which constituted the ill-defined Russian border, and he rode alone across the Carpathian Mountains into Hungary. He intended to recover the money he had left in the keeping of Prince Sigismund, and perhaps to resume his position as a mercenary.

When he reached Hungary, however, he discovered that an undeclared truce had put an end to the fighting between Turks and Christians. He continued traveling to Graz, Austria, where Sigismund was meeting with the Archduke Ferdinand. He was given shelter and welcome along the way by officers who had served with him and remembered him, but he indicated in *True Travels* that his thoughts were still with Camallata.

9

Wʜᴇɴ John Smith reached Austria he learned that Prince Sigismund had left for Prague, so Smith was obliged to follow. In Prague he learned that Sigismund had already gone to Leipzig, in Saxony. He was now reduced to depending on charity for food and shelter, so he did not linger, but hastened on to Leipzig.

There he found not only Sigismund but the Earl of Meldritch. He was warmly welcomed. At a banquet at which he was the guest of honor he was presented, by Sigismund, with a coat of arms. This gesture made Smith a true gentleman in a class-conscious era. He wasted no time recording his coat of arms in the official Register of Heraldry when he returned to England the following year.

Sigismund also presented him with a thousand ducats, to which the Earl of Meldritch added another five hundred. He also received a safe-conduct, which ruling kings and princes were required by custom to honor. With this he could safely travel through the nations of Europe.

Smith took a leisurely tour of Europe, lodging at the best inns and eating at the best taverns, enjoying himself. In Siena, Italy, he met his old friend, Henry Willoughby, who accompanied him for a while. But Henry left him in France, and Smith went on alone into Spain, anxious to visit the country that had recently been England's great enemy. He enjoyed his trip and recorded his impressions of Spain in *True Travels.*

Southern Spain faced Morocco across a narrow strip of the Mediterranean. The nearness of the Moslem world reminded Smith of Elizabeth Rondee, who had been his fellow captive in Constantinople. Perhaps it was the memory of someone who had tried to befriend him, or perhaps it was boredom with the easy life of tourism —for whatever reason, Smith decided to rescue her.

Smith knew she was the slave of the wife of the pasha of El Araish, an Atlantic port later called Larache, about fifty miles from Tangier. This area of Islam, the Barbary, was ruled by the Moors, Spain's ancient enemies, under the overlordship of the Ottomans. Unlike that of the Turks, Moroccan culture was in decline. Corruption was rife among the beys, or rulers, and pashas had been sent from Constantinople to oversee each district.

Portuguese merchant ships occasionally put in to El Araish to buy the wine that was a major product of the region. The grape growers of the area paid little attention to the injunctions in the Koran against the use of spirits. The captains of these same Portuguese ships also frequented the taverns of Spanish ports, which gave Smith a chance to question them.

Unfortunately, they knew nothing of an English captive in El Araish, but they did give Smith an accurate idea of the fortifications of the place. The town was protected by two forts on the terraced cliffs directly above the port. The Kibibat, an extension of an ancient Roman fort, was used only as a garrison, but the relatively new fortress, La Cigogne, was only twenty-five

46

years old, protected by cannon and slings. It had been built by the Portuguese themselves during their occupation of the town, and it was virtually impregnable. Mahomet ben Arif, the pasha, lived there. The Portuguese seamen with whom Smith talked held a very low opinion of the man.

For six months, claims Smith in *True Travels*, he enjoyed spectacular adventures on an English man-of-war and a Spanish privateer, furthering his education as a sailor. Unfortunately no other records exist of these vessels or of their captains, the English Merham or the Spanish Cordoba. Smith claims to have taken part, with them, in heated naval engagements.

Eventually, however, Smith arrived in El Araish, attired in magnificent robes and accompanied by eight retainers, who were in fact mercenary soldiers. They all wore armor beneath their flowing robes and carried concealed weapons. Smith greeted the harbor master in perfect Turkish and informed him that he wanted to pay his respects to Mahomet ben Arif and give that worthy a valuable gift.

Mahomet ben Arif, a bored, overweight, middle-age man, was delighted to receive the ruling prince of one of the distant German states, as Smith presented himself. He was also delighted to receive the "costly" ring, actually glass, that Smith gave him, and he invited his guests to eat with him.

During the course of the meal Smith broached the subject of the English slave, expressing delicate doubt that the pasha could own such a valuable possession. The pasha, of course, responded by summoning Elizabeth. When she appeared, Smith asked for permission to question her.

Elizabeth recognized Smith and could not contain her tears. A bloody fight ensued. Smith claims to have killed not only the pasha but a giant Moor of the pasha's guard, and the captain of the guard. Between them, Smith and his men were able to subdue all opposition. Only one of Smith's Spanish mercenaries was dead.

Smith wrapped Elizabeth in a cloak and gave her the dead Spaniard's hat and sword to complete her disguise. They then rode out of the citadel the way they had entered, with nine horses and nine riders.

They were discovered. A thundering, dramatic chase through the twisting streets of the ancient city resulted, while inhabitants scattered and pistol shots rang out behind. They reached the shore, clambered into a boat, and rowed out to Smith's vessel, which unfortunately was still at anchor, with sails furled.

After frantic labor the ship was ready to put out to sea, Smith having awakened the captain from his lethargy. By this time the gunners on the ramparts of La Cigogne had their cannons trained on the ship. Only their poor marksmanship, claims Smith in *True Travels,* saved the privateer.

The little ship easily escaped its Moorish pursuers and safety reached Cádiz. Eventually Smith was able to secure passage on a Portuguese bark that would take them to England, as no English ships could be found in the Spanish ports, and no Spanish captain was willing to sail to England as long as the peace was still only informal. On October 4, 1605, the Portuguese ship *Leonora* sailed up the Thames to London.

10

Smith's reputation was made. His countrymen were delighted with his exploits, and he visited his favorite taverns in a happy blaze of glory. He also called on Richard Hakluyt, the great geographer-scientist, who was grateful for Smith's information on Russia, as little was known of that country. And he found occasion to renew his acquaintance with Henry, Prince of Wales.

The Prince was the most popular member of the royal family, a handsome young man who often ate in taverns with the merchant class, endearing himself to the people. He was an extraordinary young man with an insatiable curiosity, vitally interested in exploration and British expansion overseas. Had he lived, he would have made a far better king than his younger brother, who became Charles I.

It was unfortunate for Smith that he and Henry should become especially friendly at a time when the Prince was in the bad graces of his father, the moody James I. In later years James forgot why he did not care for Smith, but he never forgot the grudge. Smith, in fact, was not even aware that he had made an enemy.

Smith was delighted with his new friendship with the

49

Prince of Wales. He was seen in Henry's company at several London taverns, including the famous Whitefriars, which burned to the ground in the Great Fire. In a short time he was also seen with the Dukes of Buckingham and Norfolk, and his future was considered very bright indeed.

Part of this future consisted of speculation on the part of his friends that he would soon marry Elizabeth Rondee. Her dramatic rescue from slavery made a magnificent story, as did her earlier attempts to befriend him in Constantinople. But what seemed to others to be a natural ending to the story did not appear in the same light to the two participants. In the following year Elizabeth married a prominent landowner and country squire, Sir Philip Graham. The couple remained close friends with Smith and invested a large sum of money in the company he helped form for colonizing the New World.

Smith was enjoying too much success to consider marriage, even had there been someone he wished to marry. His company was so sought after and his fame spread so rapidly that even Sir Walter Raleigh, who was being held in the Tower of London by the ever-suspicious James on grounds of treason, expressed a desire to meet him.

Just prior to Christmas 1605, Smith was summoned to Whitehall for an audience with Queen Anne. The frowzy Queen and her ladies were captivated by Smith's storytelling, even weeping sympathetically over his troubles. By the time he left, Smith had made another important friend.

This friendship rubbed even more salt in King James's emotional wounds, but Smith was not aware of it. Nor did he realize how much his attitude toward Sir Walter

Raleigh could hurt him. Smith found a kindred spirit in Sir Walter, and he ignored the stigma that attached to the Admiral after his ludicrous trial for treason. Sir Walter listened avidly to Smith's stories, recognizing a natural friend.

The influence worked both ways. Raleigh related endless stories of the New World, and Smith's fertile imagination was fired. Smith continued to pay visits to the Tower, despite Henry Hudson's warning that his activities were being reported to the King. Even though Smith later paid for his relation with Sir Walter, he never regretted it.

Late in the autumn of 1605 he paid a visit to his mother's grave in Lincolnshire. He missed her sorely, but he no longer felt very close to his other relatives, who bored him with their provincial outlook. Smith's brother Francis had named his eldest child after him, however, and Smith gave the child a scimitar, which was handed down in the family for generations. Many fictitious legends, of which Smith would have been proud, were told about the heirloom.

Smith visited his sister, Alice, and her husband, a farmer, and then visited other childhood companions. The Willoughbys were still away from home, and his other friends had grown narrow-minded. Smith paid several visits to his mother's grave, then left Lincolnshire for London.

The spirit of excitement in London suited Smith best. People were awakening to the profit in store for those willing to risk investment in overseas exploration. Since the time of Henry VII, British sea captains had sailed to previously unknown lands, yet other nations were taking the lead in colonization. National pride, which had risen to a height under Elizabeth I, demanded that the British make up for lost time.

Raleigh's expedition, among others, had laid the groundwork by establishing a British claim to the lands between the Spanish colonies in Central and South America and the French in Canada. Queen Elizabeth's East India Company had been earning profits since its chartering in 1600, and there was a clamor to expand trade. A group of London investors formed the Muscovy Company in 1606, under Hakluyt's influence. They believed that a sea passage to the East Indies could be found, and that Henry Hudson, whose views coincided with their own, was the man to do it. In 1607 Hudson sailed for the Muscovy Company on the first of his three great voyages of exploration.

Others preferred to concentrate on North America, and the possibilities that permanent settlements there would afford. Hakluyt lent his influence to this project also, as did the Prince of Wales. These men were undeterred by Raleigh's failure; King James, jealous of the success of the French and Spanish, agreed with them.

The Royal Virginia Company was formed for the purpose of exploring and settling North America, with Sir John Popham, the Lord Chief Justice, as its President. The first to purchase stock was Prince Henry, and John Smith followed with an investment of five hundred pounds, a large sum. The company soon had so many investors that it had more money than it needed.

A quarrel among the directors of the company soon resulted, with some of them wanting to concentrate their efforts in the north of the area while others preferred to establish colonies farther south. Eventually a compromise was reached by dividing the group in two. The second group, preferring to concentrate on the southern region—which became known as Virginia—called itself the London Company.

The directors applied to the King for a patent. James, surly because the directors had not consulted him when they made their plans, delayed for months. He finally granted the patent only after alarmed citizens told him the British might lose their claim if he delayed longer.

The northern branch was dogged by troubles. Hoping to send out an expedition in 1607, it bought unseaworthy ships, hired troublemakers, and lost supplies in a storm. When the expedition finally did set sail, in 1608, its leader, John Popham's brother, died at sea. The rest of the expedition spent a few weeks in a bleak land, probably a New England beach, and then gave up and returned home.

The London Company investors were more cautious, although they had set multiple goals for themselves. Believing, like most people of the time, that North America was a narrow strip of land, they expected to find a navigable river across it leading to the Pacific Ocean. They also intended to set up a colony in Virginia, and to send out parties to occupy as much territory as possible in the name of the British Crown.

They hired Captain Christopher Newport, a competent seaman, to be commodore of the Virginia fleet. Newport knew his business and engaged Bartholomew Gosnold as his deputy. Gosnold was younger and a little more impetuous; he had already made a successful voyage of discovery to the New World in 1602. The Company also hired Newport's former mate, John Ratcliffe. Captain Ratcliffe was extremely handsome, with blond hair and blue eyes. He was eager to please, and the directors had no way of knowing that his competence was handicapped by moodiness and violent fits of anger.

Three ships were purchased for the expedition: Newport's flagship, the square-rigged *Susan Constant*, large enough to carry seventy passengers and many supplies; Gosnold's older *God Speed*; and Ratcliffe's small, twenty-ton pinnace, the *Discovery*.

Smith fully intended to be a member of the expedition, right from the start, and the directors were delighted. He was a proven soldier who knew about the sea, and a recognized leader of men. He helped the three captains supervise buying supplies, and inspected all the merchandise himself, as he realized that merchants would sell inferior goods, even rotting canvas and spoiled food, if they could.

He was joined by what became the high command of the expedition. First among these men was Edward Maria Wingfield, an earnest, austere, and dedicated gentleman who unfortunately bungled everything he undertook. He was patrician and patriotic, which endeared him to the directors, but he was narrow-minded and self-righteous, and later proved a liability to the expedition.

Master George Percy, bearer of a proud name but a notorious playboy, became a member because of the influence of his brother, the Earl of Northumberland, one of the Company's directors. The Earl wanted his brother out of England, and Percy was amiable and willing to go.

Not much is known about Captain John Martin. He had been an artillery officer and was honest and dedicated. He was also in poor health and quite frail.

The Reverend Robert Hunt wanted no part in the secular affairs of the colony. He was pious and retiring but had great strength and courage and was a significant moral force in the expedition,

Captain George Kendal obtained a place for himself through the offices of his friend Ratcliffe. He was a former infantry officer, silent and vindictive. He made no friends, and his active attempts at troublemaking eventually resulted in his execution.

Last of the command was Captain Gabriel Archer, a baronet's youngest son, whose father had bought a commission for him. He had served briefly with his regiment and then fought as a mercenary in the Netherlands. He was commanding and flamboyant, although rash, and it was almost inevitable that he and Smith should clash.

The total number of the expedition came to 150 volunteers, including bricklayers, carpenters, stonemasons, sailors, and even boys still in their teens. There was no lack of volunteers.

Smith, along with Gosnold and Newport, supervised loading of the ships' stores, which included rice and oatmeal (wheat and rye spoiled easily and so were not taken); kegs of prunes, raisins, and spices; nuts, jellies, marmalades, and sea biscuits. Pickled beef, salt pork, and fish were loaded, too. Beer and cider were the bulk of the liquid refreshments taken. Although Newport and Gosnold carried casks of water, it was strictly for emergency use only. No one would dream of drinking it were anything else available.

Detailed instructions on every conceivable matter were prepared by the directors. The type of government the colonists were to establish was outlined, as were guidelines for the treatment of natives. Unfortunately these orders were drawn up at a secret meeting and given in a locked box to Captain Newport, with instructions not to open it until the New World was reached. This was intended to prevent rivalry among the would-be leaders on the long voyage, but the lack of instructions and a specific chain of command instead created confusion and dissension.

 **11**

Smith was happy during the year 1606. He was helping supervise supplying the expedition, and his popularity was undimmed. He went to taverns mainly to enjoy the conversation and to be admired, which he was. He also had a mistress, Frances, Duchess of Richmond, one of the most glamorous and intelligent women in England. The affair was common knowledge, but Frances's husband, Ludovic Stuart, one of Scotland's leading gentlemen, did not mind, an attitude in keeping with the times. He was quite happy to amuse himself elsewhere.

Frances was a sophisticated woman who enjoyed the limelight and being the center of attention, a pastime that occasionally included shocking the pious Queen Anne. Frances had no children and devoted a great deal of time to charity. She had a sincere interest in the poor, and they, in turn, developed a great affection for her. In an age when women were mostly charming decorations, she was well educated and unafraid of showing it. She was a student of philosophy and the natural sciences and a witty conversationalist. Smith enjoyed her company, and she was happy to be seen with the man who was probably the most traveled Englishman of the age, who

57

had been in Islam, Central Europe, the Carpathians, and even the closed society of Russia.

By the end of the year Smith was too busy to see much of the Duchess, however. The date for the great voyage was drawing nearer, and preparations were becoming hectic. Smith's relations with the directors were also becoming strained.

The directors nourished vast hopes of the wealth to be gained from the New World, wealth in the form of gold, diamonds, and emeralds by the shipload. Smith, however willing he might be to exaggerate his own merits, was pragmatic in this case. The Spanish, he was convinced, had made off with all the gold and jewels to be had, since in almost one hundred years no one else had returned from the Americas with wealth in that form. He believed in the natural raw resources of North America, and in the value of establishing colonies. He also had to dissuade the council from its wild plans of colonizing the South Seas. The expedition, he insisted, would have its hands full establishing a settlement in Virginia.

The expedition was to sail on January 1, 1607. On the last day of the year 1606 Smith dined with Prince Henry and Richard Hakluyt, then went to Whitehall for a formal audience with the King, as did the other leaders. King James, sick and lethargic, made a few remarks and cut the interview short. He did not and would not realize the importance of the expedition.

At dawn on New Year's Day, 1607, the clergyman of the expedition, Robert Hunt, delivered three sermons at communion services in Westminster Abbey. The entire company attended, as did most members of the council and their families. The whole party then went down to the wharves on the Thames where the three ships were docked.

The weather was foul, but a number of the directors made their planned speeches anyway, standing in strong winds under a sky that threatened snow. A final inspection of the ships by the directors and their families was in progress when the wind suddenly shifted. Captain Newport immediately cut short the celebrations, declaring that the favorable winds should not be wasted. All hands were piped aboard, and the three ships set sail down the Thames.

Smith, along with the other gentlemen, was aboard the *Susan Constant.* Unfortunately he had to share his tiny cabin with Gabriel Archer, with whom he was least likely to be compatible. Each wanted to be the sole leader of the expedition, and they soon became bitter enemies.

Rivalries were still in the future, however, and the weather remained fine as they continued down the Thames. One small incident set the stage for times to come. Someone leaked the news that Captain Ratcliffe of the *Discovery* had once served a prison term under the name of Sicklemore. No one knew the nature of his offense, and the times being what they were, no one was concerned. The problem arose when someone told Ratcliffe that he had been exposed. Smith was named as the tattletale, with the added hint that he asked that Ratcliffe be sent ashore. No action was taken, of course.

Smith was innocent of spreading gossip, and at a later time others were to claim that he was not responsible. Smith suspected that Archer was the troublemaker, but by then the damage was done. Ratcliffe had joined the ranks of Smith's enemies.

The weather worsened and the ships could not even move out into the English Channel. Winter gales forced them to anchor in the Downs. Impatience grew as the wait lengthened, and men were sent ashore in small boats for supplies. The waiting continued for six weeks, during which time Archer, Kendal, and Ratcliffe continued to work against Smith.

Smith, of course, was more than partly to blame for this situation. With his customary lack of modesty he was making it plain that he would act as military leader when the expedition reached Virginia. His self-esteem was so great that he took it for granted that others must feel the same way about him. He even managed to irritate the placid Wingfield. Eventually only Percy and Martin remained friendly with him.

The Reverend Hunt also became Smith's loyal ally, due to a circumstance in which Smith gave him much needed support. Hunt became ill during the long wait, so ill that Newport considered sending him home. Hunt refused to leave, expressing determination to sail with the others. Smith backed him in his decision. When Hunt recovered he remained Smith's staunch friend.

Finally, in February, the weather changed and Newport ordered them to set sail for the Canary Islands, which they reached without incident. There they took on supplies of fresh water and meat, as some of their stewed mutton had spoiled. Many of the passengers were restless and unhappy, and there was some talk of turning back. But the grumbling ceased when the little flotilla made ready to sail across the Atlantic.

Although the grumbling may have diminished with the sailing, the boredom did not. Trouble among the men increased, and Smith, bored also, did nothing to stop it. Archer and Kendal continued to snipe at him, and one day, so Smith claims in *A True Relation*, they called him "names so foul that no man could tolerate such abuse." He drew his sword. Archer and Kendal, declaring complete innocence, said that Smith drew without cause. Captain Newport had to intervene to end the fracas.

On the following day Wingfield was persuaded to preside over a makeshift "court of inquiry" to determine Smith's punishment. There was no doubt as to the motivating forces behind the "court," and Newport and his officers refused to have any part in it. The court, led by Archer and Kendal, voted to hang Smith as soon as they reached land. Smith probably could have put everything straight by gravely apologizing, even though he did not believe himself to be in the wrong. He did not, however. Instead, he did the worst thing possible. He laughed. All chances of reconciliation were lost.

 **12**

O<small>N</small> March 24 they cast anchor off the island of Hispaniola in the Caribbean. The island was Columbus's initial landing place, and as such was claimed by Spain. But the only Spaniards there were missionaries, all of them living inland. To the sea-weary English, the island seemed a lush paradise. Everyone went ashore.

Almost immediately Carib Indians appeared from the jungles, all of them shy and friendly. It was not long before bartering had begun, the English trading beads, hatchets, and knives for fresh-killed meat—in particular, wild boar—and fish, as well as strange fruits. Trade in alcohol or firearms was forbidden, a policy the British were to adhere to, at least officially, in all their New World colonizing ventures.

John Smith was seated on the beach earnestly attempting to learn the language of the Caribs from some of the obliging natives when he noticed some hard labor in progress among his shipmates. They were building a gallows. It was obvious that his enemies had not forgotten the "sentence" they had passed on him.

In due time the gallows was completed. Archer and Kendal then had to proceed to the next step: taking

Smith into custody and hanging him. Smith made no attempt to run away. He simply waited for them to come and get him, in light armor and a helmet, despite the heat, and bristling with weapons: his scimitar, a sharp smallsword, a brace of dueling pistols in his belt, and a knife protruding from his boot top. It occurred to the adventurers that he had come ashore prepared.

Under the circumstances they began to have second thoughts about the propriety of the death sentence. They realized that any man who tried to take Smith would be risking death himself, and it was doubtful that even several of them could do the job. In any case, no one wanted to be first.

Captain Newport was aware of the foolishness of the plan, and with the Reverend Hunt as an ally he had no trouble dissuading the others from carrying it out. Smith, recounting the incident in *A True Relation,* was scornful. "I . . . knew that there was no swordsman in that miserable lot who could stand up to me with impunity," he wrote. The entire company then settled down amicably to watch a spectacle in the harbor: a fight between a large swordfish and a small whale. After a couple of hours of this, the Indians canoed out and disposed of both fish and mammal, bringing them back for a feast.

On March 27 the ships put out to sea again, then anchored off the shores of Guadeloupe. There they inspected a hot spring and a geyser, and Smith and Martin went hunting for wild boar, shooting two. The company cooked the pork in the waters of the hot springs, and Smith's boar was enjoyed by the commoners, with whom his popularity increased. Most of the gentlemen of the expedition, however, remained cool toward him.

Two days later the ships visited Nevis Island. Natives

were seen hiding in the jungles behind the beach, and landing parties went ashore armed. Smith arbitrarily took command, without even considering Archer's claim that he should be the military leader. The Indians had no intention of attacking, however, and the stay on Nevis was peaceful.

Nevis was more than peaceful; it seemed like a paradise. The men spent six days there, washing their clothes and bathing in the mineral springs, gathering an abundance of wild fruits and berries and thus incidentally staving off scurvy. Fish and game were plentiful, even tropical deer, and the whole company enjoyed venison, which in England had become a food primarily of the upper classes. Spirits rose to such an extent that Percy even went to Smith with an apology, although Kendal and Archer refused to consider making peace.

On April 3 they set sail once again, and on the following day reached the Virgin Islands. On the Island of Saint Eustatius they snared an abundance of fowl and caught fish and a 280-pound turtle. They also saw an iguana, which Smith, in a fit of disgust, killed and threw into a sand pit. After two days, when they had found no fresh water, they left Saint Eustatius and stopped at islands, otherwise unidentified, which they called Mona and Moneta. There they took on fresh water in place of the water they had taken at Nevis, which unaccountably developed a horrible smell.

It was on one of these small islands that the company had its first loss. A portly gentleman named Edward Brookes died in the jungle from overexertion and heat. He was buried with military honors, but even his funeral did not greatly lower the company's spirits. Scores of birds were killed, and the nests of the birds were discov-

64

ered, giving the company fresh eggs for the first time since they had left England. Clear freshwater springs were also found, enabling them to replenish their water supply. On April 10 they sailed north again, and four days later were just east of the southern tip of Florida, a Spanish enclave.

Trouble arrived, not in the form of the Spanish but as a fierce gale. For a full week they fought the storm, losing much gear overboard. Most passengers were seasick, but Smith remained active. On April 22 the weather finally cleared; by then Newport could not find his position, and the ships were lost.

Soundings were taken, and based on his findings Newport believed he had been blown hopelessly far out into the Atlantic. In actuality he was probably just off the North American continental shelf, but he had no way of knowing it. After three days of continuous westward sailing they still had not sighted land. Newport called a meeting on board the *Susan Constant*, where Ratcliffe proposed to his fellow captains that they return to England.

Smith was violent in opposing this idea. If they returned to England months would go by before the expedition could be refitted, and most of the settlers would probably lose heart and have to be replaced. Even more dire was the possibility that the investors might withdraw their financial support. Smith proposed that if they continued to sail westward they would eventually find land. Newport seconded this motion, and the ships continued their westward course. Although Smith was responsible for this decision, it had been worded in his usual arrogant fashion, and Archer, Ratcliffe, and Kendal hated him even more.

On April 25 they ran into another gale. The captains made no attempt to fight it, only staying within hailing distance of one another. Most of the company felt sure they were now hopelessly lost. But when the wind died, a sailor in the crow's nest of the *Susan Constant* reported land, to everyone's amazement and relief.

A few hours later Newport led his ships into what Smith would later name Chesapeake Bay. The shore party was delighted by the pleasant meadows, brooks, and tall trees and decided to spend the night on land, intending to continue explorations in the morning.

That night the Indians attacked. Approaching silently out of the forest, they sent a hail of arrows against the unprepared English. Mathew Morton, a sailor, was seriously injured in the initial assault. Smith, who was with the landing party, ordered his fellows away from the fire, where they made targets outlined by the flames. Captain Newport fired his musket and pistols; the Indians, who had never heard the sound of firearms, scattered.

The next morning, April 27, Newport decided at last that it was time to open the instructions the directors had given him in London. A council of seven was to govern the colony. The seven the directors had chosen included the three ships' captains—Newport, Gosnold, and Ratcliffe—and four gentlemen: Edward Wingfield, John Martin, George Kendal, and John Smith. They were instructed to hold office for one year and to elect their own president. A majority vote was to decide all major questions, with the president getting two votes and the others having one apiece.

Had the instructions been read at the beginning of the voyage much trouble could have been avoided, but now it was too late. Ratcliffe and Kendal refused to allow

Smith to take his seat on the council, and they persuaded Gosnold and Wingfield to support their position. Newport and Martin supported Smith, but Smith's arrogance had alienated too many. Rather than see a fight break out, Smith did not press his right, accepting the decision of the majority although he made it clear that he did so only temporarily.

Construction of a shallow-water vessel began for the navigation of rivers. The shallop, later to be called a sloop, could carry twenty-five men. Double-masted and clumsy-looking, it did not greatly resemble modern sloops, but it was a useful little vessel. While others worked on its construction, Smith took some of the company with him on an eight-mile march into the forest. They discovered a store of fresh oysters that undoubtedly belonged to the Indians, but had no compunction about appropriating the shellfish for themselves. They also found and devoured a profusion of wild strawberries.

The shallop was completed on April 28. Newport took it for a brief sail on the lower part of Chesapeake Bay, with most of the gentlemen accompanying him. Oysters and mussels were everywhere, and everyone ate his fill. A permanent anchorage was found at the mouth of what was to be called the James River, and Smith drew his first sketches of the area. These would later be included in his remarkably accurate maps.

Smith suggested that the peninsula at the southern end of the bay be named Cape Henry, after the Prince of Wales. On April 29 they erected a cross on Cape Henry, marking their presence. The land was pleasant and the climate warm, although the sea breezes moderated the temperature at night. The sandy beaches yielded many oysters, mussels, and clams, the latter a species unknown in Europe. The huge forests were impressive, and the soil was declared excellent for farming.

A large group of natives was seen on April 30 at Point Comfort, a point of land at the mouth of the James River, and Newport ordered the shallop to cross and meet with them.

Smith stood in the bow of the ship and pantomimed friendship. Although the men with him had weapons, they were well hidden. The warriors outnumbered the English and held their ground. Smith was the first to leap ashore, and in *A True Relation* he presents himself as flinging handfuls of beads. The warriors must have been astonished at such a peculiar sight, but Smith says they eagerly snatched the gifts.

The encounter was a success, and soon the two parties were sitting down to eat together. The menu included venison, cornbread, and a great delicacy, roast dog. It was a good thing the English did not realize the nature of the pièce de résistance until near the end of the meal; they thought they were eating roast pork. Smith insisted that they hide their revulsion, however, and thus managed to keep Anglo-Indian relations on an even keel.

The biggest and best surprise came when the warriors lighted pipes and passed them to their guests. Tobacco brought such a good price in England that it was known as "green gold," and Smith was delighted to know that it could be grown in the area.

One of the main purposes of the expedition was to find a water passage to the Pacific. All the educated members of the expedition firmly believed that this ocean was only a short distance away, two or three hundred miles at most, and that there must be a river connecting it with the Atlantic. Now that the friendship of the local tribe had been won, they were determined to explore inland and find this passage.

On May 4 Smith took a party of exploration up the James River in the shallop. They stopped at a large Indian village called Paspahegh, where Smith and Percy spent some time trying to learn the language. Although the men of Smith's party believed firmly in the natural superiority of English ways, the Indians had a level of civilization sufficiently impressive to fascinate them.

The Indians farmed extensively, living in villages of about one hundred inhabitants to well over one thousand. Clans were matrilineal: women owned the houses and the land. A man moved into his wife's house upon marriage, but he spent some of his time each day in a longhouse reserved as the exclusive gathering place of the men. Children lived with their mothers until they wished to leave, and frequently did not: extended families often lived in one large longhouse with several cooking hearths.

Smith learned the language rapidly and discovered that the town was headquarters of the local chief, named Powhatan. Smith soon knew enough of the language to speak directly with Powhatan, learning that the man was chief sachem of the whole Chickahominy Confederation, which encompassed many tribes. He was greatly disturbed by the mention of nations living far to the west, however, and for the first time began to suspect that the continent was larger than they had originally thought, and that the chances of finding a water passage to the Pacific were greatly reduced.

Smith and Percy remained with Powhatan when the others returned to the shallop for the night, and they

69

were the guests at a feast the Chickahominy gave for them. Smith praised the cornbread so much that Powhatan presented him with several baskets of corn kernels, and even gave him planting instructions. Smith's insistence that the colonists follow these directions helped prevent famine during their first winter.

The Chickahominy were a handsome people who loved ornamentation, although this included a predilection for bear grease and red ochre, which both men and women loved to smear in their hair. Powhatan had a cape of magnificent feathers that stretched all the way to the ground. When Smith expressed his admiration of it, the chief graciously gave him one like it, a gesture that was to produce great jealousy among the other gentlemen.

If Smith met Powhatan's young daughter Pocahontas during this visit, he does not mention it in *A True Relation* or in *The Generall Historie of Virginia.* Although she held a high rank in her tribe, she was still a child, and it is unlikely that Smith would have noticed her. He would not, of course, have been accustomed to thinking of little girls as important, but in view of the romantic furor he made in later years, his omission of her name may be significant.

On May 5 Smith and Percy returned to their party in the shallop, which continued its trip up-river. Powhatan had sent word ahead, and they were well received at several villages. Smith continued efforts to learn the Chickahominy language. Finally, at the village of Appamatuck, far upstream, the river narrowed. It was obvious that this was not the Pacific passage, and the shallop turned back.

On May 13 the shallop returned to the ships. Smith, who was still refused his seat on the council, made his report only to Captain Newport, an act that further increased the hostility against him. On the following day the ships sailed up the James to a point near Powhatan's town. There they went ashore and began building houses, a meeting hall, and a fort.

Work was still in progress when Powhatan appeared, surrounded by warriors, all heavily smeared with ceremonial paint. They brought with them the carcasses of several deer and were obviously ready for a feast. Smith hastily donned his feather cloak and went to meet the sachem. From Smith's actions it is likely that Powhatan thought him the war-chief of the English, which, of course, is exactly what Smith wanted to be.

Others were not agreed on this designation, and as the feast progressed, Archer and Kendal in particular became more and more irritated by Smith's manner. Wingfield, who had just been elected president of the council, insisted on making a long-winded speech to the Indians. Smith was the only one who could translate, and he did so with such brevity that Wingfield became annoyed. Smith said blandly that he did not yet know enough of the language to make a full translation. Wingfield had never had a good opinion of Smith, and this incident added further fuel to his hostility.

Just before dusk, when the Indians were about to leave, one of the English discovered a brave either examining or stealing his ax. The Englishman assumed it was theft and threatened to beat the culprit's brains out, with gestures so clear they needed no translation. Everyone began shouting at once, and the English ran for their muskets while Powhatan gathered his warriors around him.

Although order was restored, Powhatan was angry at

the breach of hospitality. It is possible that he felt that if the warrior admired the ax he should be given it, or one like it, just as Smith had been given a feather cloak. This would have been only natural courtesy. But the English had threatened violence, and Powhatan made it clear that, with the exception of John Smith, he no longer considered them his friends.

13

Powhatan was no longer friendly to the colonists, and they were torn by dissension. Other quarrels than those with Smith soon erupted. Under the circumstances it is a wonder the colony survived at all.

Wingfield, the poorest possible choice for president of the council, did not approve of the site chosen for the settlement. In his inexperience he declared it was both inaccessible and difficult to defend. Gosnold laughed at him, comparing Jamestown's deep-water channel with that of London. Furthermore, palisades were being built around the town, and cannon would be placed in the fort. Jamestown would be well defended.

Wingfield at first took umbrage at Gosnold, but later, in a furious dispute with Archer, changed his mind. Archer had been spoiling for a fight ever since he had learned that he was excluded from the council by the orders of the directors. He told Wingfield that he was sure he had been left out of those consulted on the possible sites for the town because Wingfield had disapproved of the sketches he had drawn up while on board the *Discovery*. Archer must have been very naïve to believe that he could draw up plans for a town's defenses before he even knew its location. Wingfield countered with the arguments he had just recently heard from Gosnold.

Even more serious was the difference of opinion between Wingfield and the rest of the council. Afraid of further offending Powhatan, he ordered the construction of both the fort and the palisades to be halted. Only Kendal's defense system, an intertwining of tree branches, more decorative than useful, was permitted. Wingfield had two votes, and Kendal of course sided with him. Ratcliffe joined them, out of dislike for Gosnold and Newport.

This brought the council to a deadlock, with four votes in favor of completing the palisades and four in favor of Kendal's scheme. Had Smith been seated on the council as the directors intended, no tie would have been possible. Under the circumstances Wingfield declared that his wishes would be observed, since they could not be vetoed. For a while impeachment was considered by some of the men, but Smith and Newport, afraid of open rebellion, calmed them with promises that construction of the fortifications would soon be resumed. They were convinced that Wingfield would change his stance, given time.

He did just that, and construction resumed on May 19. Smith and Newport became, in the popular mind, leaders of the colony. The commoners in particular sought Smith's advice.

Smith set himself the task of teaching everyone how to load, fire, and clean muskets, as there were many in the company who were unfamiliar with the use of firearms. It seemed obvious that all the colonists should know both how to hunt and how to defend themselves. Wingfield did not like the plan, claiming that Smith was trying to gain favor with the commoners, which in fact he had already done. He was ordered to cease the "exercises." Nonetheless, supported by Newport, he quietly continued them.

In late May another party of men began a trip of exploration up the James River. Newport took command of the twenty-three men but gave Smith command of the land party that was to explore the forest whenever the shallop landed. Smith's account of this journey appears in *A True Relation*. George Percy and Archer also kept accounts of the voyage, but Smith's is possibly the best.

The party traveled about seventy miles up the James River, the same distance that Smith had previously covered. This time, however, the journey was made at a much slower pace, with frequent pauses so that Smith could take his group inland into the forests.

They met often with Indians from some of the tribes of Powhatan's loose confederation. Smith, however obnoxious he was to his peers, had a knack for winning frienship of the natives, and he put it to good use. When they stopped at Paspahegh, which they felt obliged to do, Smith made strenuous efforts to heal the rift with the sachem.

He presented Powhatan with a number of gifts: brass bells, shears, and his own razor. Powhatan had little use for this last item; he was used to plucking his sparse beard with tweezers, as was the native custom. Nonetheless, he was both pleased and mollified.

Even more important, Smith brought out paper, ink, and a quill pen, and drew a rough sketch of the river and territory as he knew it. Powhatan caught the idea immediately, and indicated where changes should be made. Smith gave him the writing implements also.

Powhatan sent guides along with them, one of them

his own son. The party stopped frequently at Indian communities along the way. Every time they stopped the Indians gave them a feast, and Smith took the opportunity to sample more of the foods peculiar to the New World. He was particularly delighted by maple syrup and blueberries.

They went as far inland as the site of what was to become Richmond. There Newport optimistically claimed all territory as far as the Pacific Ocean in the name of the Crown, and erected a cross on a hillside. An inscription was burned into the wood informing all who could read it that the land belonged to the English.

The party took its time in returning to Jamestown. The forest was pleasant, and they enjoyed identifying the trees and wildflowers they knew, and giving names to those they did not. Smith made it his business to learn more about the edible plants and roots of the region, questioning his Indian guides.

When they finally reached Jamestown they discovered they were just too late to avert tragedy. On the previous day a band of Chesapeake Indians, unaffiliated with Powhatan's confederacy, had made a surprise attack on the town. Wingfield had been totally unprepared for the emergency. The defenses were still incomplete. Even worse, most of the settlers had been caught unarmed outside the walls where they had been scattered over a wide area sowing corn when the attack came. Although Smith had insisted that those traveling outside the compound carry a musket, Wingfield had forbidden anyone to carry any arms at all.

The colonists were lucky. Most had managed to run to safety within the walls. Twelve had been wounded; two, one a young boy, had been killed. Gosnold had unlimbered the cannon on the three ships, and their roar, more than any damage they inflicted, had frightened off the natives. All the council members except Wingfield had been wounded, and the settlement was in an uproar.

Smith assumed that the Chesapeakes would return, and many agreed with him. He insisted that the colony be better prepared. Wingfield stubbornly refused permission for the fortifications to be completed, but this time he was ignored. The commoners sided with Smith and set to work immediately.

Within the next three weeks the Chesapeake made four separate raids, all at night, two after sundown and two just before dawn. They shot flaming arrows into the town in the hope of starting a fire that would drive the defenders out. But Smith was ready for them now. There were sentries on duty twenty-four hours a day, and any Indian who approached the town stealthily was fired upon.

Wingfield was not pleased. Despite the obvious danger, he insisted on a policy of pacification. Apparently it did not occur to him that he could not pacify everyone: if Jamestown were allied with Powhatan, then Powhatan's enemies were Jamestown's enemies also.

Most of the company stood by Smith. Only Kendal, Ratcliffe, and Wingfield were against him. Two more settlers were killed during the third and fourth raids, and after the last death the whole colony rebelled. Percy and Martin drew up a petition demanding that the council be reformed, and even Archer signed it. Wingfield, faced with open rebellion, surrendered. On June 14 Smith was admitted to his rightful place on the council.

 **14**

Smith lost no time taking charge of the colony. The palisades were strengthened and two new towers were added to the fort. Land was cleared of brush for several hundred feet all around the town, making it impossible for an attacking enemy to keep under cover near the walls.

Smith set the men to other pursuits besides defense. The directors in London would not be satisfied with their mere survival; they wanted a profit from the colony. Tall trees were cut into lumber and stored in the holds of the ships. Smith realized the value of the sturdy New World hardwoods.

Smith was now, in effect, president of the settlement, although Wingfield still held that title officially. It was time for diplomacy, and Smith knew it. The little community had been greatly weakened by the internal dissension when they had so many other problems. Smith decided to use his considerable charm to work himself into the president's good graces. He succeeded, and Wingfield no longer felt him a threat to his office.

In late June Newport prepared to sail back to England. He felt safe in leaving the colony now that it was under Smith's direction. Artillery had been mounted at each corner of the fort, and men were drilling under Smith's instruction. He tried to placate Archer by nominating him for the post of deputy field commander and to calm Gosnold by giving him the position of artillery commander.

By the end of June the *Susan Constant* was ready to sail. Smith had just concluded a barter with Powhatan, and his end of the deal, valuable beaver and fox furs, was safely stored as cargo in Newport's hold. Although the gentlemen all made merry at Newport's farewell dinner, Smith was still worried. Before Newport left he demanded that the council meet with him for a final time.

They met in the master's cabin, where Smith presented them with some unsettling facts. Despite all the crops that had been planted, including corn, beans, and peas, there might not be enough food to see all 105 men through a Virginia winter. There was no guarantee that the crops they had planted would be good, and Newport could leave behind only limited supplies. He proposed that the council petition the directors in London for provisions. For the first time in the colony's brief history, the council was unanimous in passing a resolution. The petition was drafted then and there.

Newport reached London in mid-August. Although the directors were aware of the value of his cargo, they were disappointed because there were no precious gems aboard, and no gold. They were unwilling to give up their dreams, and prepared fresh instructions ordering an increase in the search for gems and gold. They understood the precarious conditions of the colony, however, and sent out two ships laden with provisions as rapidly as they could.

In Jamestown the situation was much worse. Wingfield, now that Newport was gone, had issued a number of "rules." Military drills were forbidden, on the grounds that they wasted ammunition, and all work on the palisades was again ordered stopped. Any man who wished to go hunting or fishing was required to have a written permit from the president.

Smith lost his temper as soon as he learned of the new rules. Other council members were unhappy too, for Wingfield had seen fit to consult no one except Kendal before issuing his instructions. Smith demanded a full council meeting to discuss the situation, but Wingfield procrastinated. Finally, the council met without him.

Wingfield learned of the meeting and stormed in, declaring that it was illegal. The others then replied that his presence made it legal. So Wingfield did attend, but with bad grace.

First priority was given to discussing defenses. Wingfield had the colonists building houses, in anticipation of the arrival of more settlers. Gosnold said this was absurd; fortifications should be built first. The others, with the exception of Kendal, agreed with him, and Wingfield was voted down.

Smith was concerned with the matter of provisions. There was only enough wheat and barley, if rationed, for another fourteen weeks. Not only that, but the sentries tended to fall asleep at night if they had too little to eat. For that reason he suggested that everyone not strictly needed in the town go out and take part in the search for food. The majority of the council agreed with him, but would have no part of his plan to trade with the Indians for food. Their recent experiences with the natives had made them too uneasy to have any dealings with them.

The council was to regret its decision. By the end of

July the weather was so hot and damp that men fainted after only moderate exertion. Game and fish fled to cooler regions. Shellfish remained, but the colonists were heartily sick of their taste.

And then sickness struck. No one knew what it was. It began with a rash and a high fever, and inflicted such a devastating weakness that the men could not work. By the end of August more than half the settlers were ill, unable to do any work.

The healthy ones now had twice as much work to do, but they too were weak from the heat and from lack of food. Smith somehow stayed healthy during this period, and rarely slept, working tirelessly to keep the colony together.

Captain Bartholomew Gosnold died of the mysterious illness on August 22, and was followed within a month by forty-five others. Smith fell ill, too, and for a time his life was in doubt. He rallied swiftly, however, to everyone's relief, and in two days was able to return to duty.

When Ratcliffe fell ill Smith nursed him faithfully. Ratcliffe had the opportunity, during this time, to think over the causes of his antagonism toward Smith. He wondered if Smith had really attacked him at the very beginning of the voyage, and he brought the matter into the open. He had a profound change of heart on learning that Smith had not slandered or attacked him.

Ratcliffe now saw Kendal as the troublemaker he was. He had a long talk with Wingfield, who, when he finally saw the light, was shocked. Wingfield called a meeting of the council at which formal charges of treason were brought against Kendal. Kendal was unanimously voted out of office, placed under arrest, and given to Smith for safekeeping. Smith had to keep Kendal in his own house

81

while a cell was built in the fort.

Due to the death of so many settlers, rations for the survivors were increased, and some of the men were strong enough to work. Smith decided it was time to visit some of Powhatan's villages. Acting on his own authority, he asked for volunteers; Ratcliffe, Percy, and eleven commoners asked to go. They took the shallop, loaded with sacks of beads and trinkets. Within three days they had returned to Jamestown, the deck of the shallop piled with baskets of corn and venison.

Smith returned to more problems. During his absence Wingfield had done it again, declaring that no one who was ill should receive any food until he was strong enough to apply for his rations in person and return to work. Martin argued viciously with the president over this order, and some of the commoners were so upset that they were threatening to lynch Wingfield.

Smith and Martin consulted with Ratcliffe, and the three council members decided that it was time to take drastic measures. They voted to depose Wingfield, place him under arrest, and replace him with Ratcliffe. They then called on Wingfield to break the news to him.

The ex-president wept when he was taken on board the *Discovery,* a move the council felt was necessary to prevent some of the upset commoners from murdering him. The sentence was harsh, for Wingfield was only a bungler, not a criminal, but it was decided to deport him to England as soon as the ships returned. The fledgling colony could afford no more errors.

One of the first tasks facing those remaining on the council was the election of new members. Smith suggested that all the gentlemen serve for terms of a few months until the London directors appointed new and permanent governors. This suggestion was accepted.

In the meantime the council decided to bring Wingfield to trial. The former president was charged with having kept alcohol for his own use, with having slandered a commoner, and with having administered the colony's affairs badly. Wingfield pleaded guilty to all but the charge of poor administration.

The council found him guilty of everything and fined him several thousand pounds. He had no money, so they seized all his personal property, which they distributed to all those he had maligned. Smith received two hundred pounds' worth of goods, which consisted of weapons and clothing. Smith found this so embarrassing that he put the goods into the community warehouse, to be used by anyone who needed them.

Now that Ratcliffe was president, he realized his own limitations as he never had before. He had few supporters, whereas Smith's popularity was high in the little community. He therefore appointed Smith as his deputy, putting him in charge of all work done outdoors.

Smith drew up schedules for everyone. Those still convalescing were put to work thatching roofs for the houses, while healthy men were expanding the clearing, working in the fields, and strengthening the fort.

Smith made another trip up the James River in the shallop, although the little ship had lost its sails in a gale and rowing was hard work, especially upstream. He visited five Indian villages, bartering axes and iron cooking pots for food. When the people of the fifth village showed no desire to trade, Smith ordered muskets fired into the air. The natives got the point, and barter was brisk.

Smith's mission was highly successful. He returned to Jamestown with thirty bushels of corn, twenty of wheat, and seventeen of so-called Indian rye. They also brought venison, wild turkeys, bear bacon, fish, oysters, and salt from a salt lick for preserving the meat they did not immediately consume. The threat of famine faded even further a few weeks later when the colonists' corn, peas, and beans ripened. Everyone was put to work harvesting, and the supplies were stored in the common warehouse, to which only Smith and Ratcliffe had keys.

In the autumn, after several more successful trips to Indian villages, Smith began to think about another problem. The settlers' clothes, which they had brought with them from England, were becoming threadbare. The supply ships from England still had not arrived, and the men had neither wool, flax, nor knowledge necessary for making shirts, breeches, and coats. In retrospect the problem does not seem so great. The obvious thing to do was to emulate the Indians.

Smith was the first to do so, curing deerskin and even buffalo hide from the occasional animal found in the interior valleys. The others refused to dress like the natives, feeling it beneath their dignity as Englishmen. As the weather grew colder, however, there was an abrupt change of heart as many found warmth preferable to fashion.

There was also the problem of Kendal. It was both inconvenient and difficult to keep him in the fort, so Radcliffe had him transferred onboard the *Discovery*. This was a mistake, as both Smith and Ratcliffe should have known from the beginning. Kendal seized the opportunity to conspire with the easily influenced Wingfield. They also managed to persuade members of the ship's crew, who took turns guarding them, that life in the New World was intolerable.

In very little time the two ex-council members had concocted a scheme to steal the ship and return to England. They proposed to do this while Smith was away from Jamestown, ignoring the fact that this would leave the little colony with no means of emergency retreat. The sailors secretly dug a tunnel into the rear of the warehouse and supplies were smuggled onto the ship. One bright October morning the sails were hoisted, and the *Discovery* prepared to leave Jamestown.

Smith, in *A True Relation*, claims this as another opportunity for his daring deeds. Returning to Jamestown in the shallop, he says, he found the *Discovery* about to depart, and Ratcliffe on the shore pleading with Kendal and Wingfield. Smith immediately ordered all the men off the *Discovery*.

Naturally, he was not obeyed. He then drew his pistol and fired two shots, grazing Kendal's ear with one of them. He also ordered the men on shore to fire at will at those on the ship. The sailors and Wingfield surrendered promptly upon hearing this command, but Kendal refused. Smith then allegedly drew his scimitar, which he happened to be wearing at the time, and, brandishing it overhead, leaped on board. He personally took Kendal into custody.

The offenses were serious enough that Smith insisted on an immediate trial. A jury of six gentlemen and six commoners was drawn up. Ratcliffe acted as the judge and Smith as the prosecutor. Kendal, as the principal conspirator, was sentenced to be hanged. So was James Read, a crewman, after he tried to attack Ratcliffe with a knife. Smith claims to have wrenched the weapon from him, thus saving Ratcliffe's life. The sentences were carried out one cold November morning, and the men took the lesson to heart. There were no more mutinies.

Smith continued to make trips of exploration and food bartering in the shallop, traveling overland as far northward as the Potomac. He made very thorough explorations. His notes on what he found were just as thorough, including not only maps but sketches of trees and comments on the nature of the soil. And he always returned with provisions.

Winter came early in 1607–8. The early cold did bring one benefit, however. Great flocks of ducks, geese, and swans flew southward from the hill country to the slightly milder climate of the coast, and an expedition from Jamestown brought down so many birds that they finally ran out of ammunition. The birds provided a welcome change in the settlers' diet.

Smith's trips were not always peaceful. On one occasion he was taken prisoner by the sachem Opechancanough, but he got out of the situation by a little fast-talking and by giving the chief his compass. He escaped two ambushes successfully, although he lost two of his men, and on one occasion he himself was captured.

His captors were those same Chesapeakes who had previously made raids against the colony, and Smith discovered they were planning a new attack. Smith was somehow able to persuade them to let him send a message to Jamestown saying that he was still alive and well. Just why the Indians would permit this is a mystery, but they did, and sent three braves to Jamestown with a note. The message said, instead, that the colony should be prepared for a major attack.

It was during this period, Smith later claimed, that he met and was saved by Pocahontas. The record is doubtful and unclear, however, and bears some examination.

15

Jᴏʜɴ sᴍɪᴛʜ's first published book, *A True Relation of such occurrences and accidents of note as hath hapned in Virginia since the first planting of that Collony*, makes no mention of Matsoaksats, or Pocahontas. Instead, he ascribes his freedom to an exhibition of artillery fire that terrified the Chesapeake messengers. Their description, in turn, so terrified their sachems that Smith was freed without further ado.

It would seem likely, at first glance, that this was indeed the course of events. *A True Relation* concerned events in Jamestown from the beginning of the expedition until June 1608, was officially registered at Stationers' Hall in London on August 13, and was published about two months later. Certainly so dramatic a rescue by Pocahontas would be considered an "accident of note" and would not be something Smith would forget to mention. Nor does Wingfield's account, published after his return to England in 1608, make reference to her. Percy is silent on the subject, as is William Simmonds, who published *The Proceedings of the English Colony in Virginia* in 1612.

The legend posterity knows is essentially the one Smith later concocted for his readers. Smith, condemned to death by Powhatan, was saved at the last minute by the brave intervention of the sachem's beautiful daughter, who begged for his life. This romantic tale was enlivened further by hints of a love affair between Englishman and Indian.

She first appears in Smith's works in the second edition of *A True Relation*, published after she arrived in England in 1617 with her husband John Rolfe. She was then the sensation of the land, and crowds followed her around London.

Smith's account of his meeting with her occurs in a series of running footnotes in the new version of *A True Relation*. The young Indian woman was at that time the favorite of Queen Anne, and even the dour James was charmed by her beauty and sweetness. She was also exceptionally intelligent, and her conversion to Christianity brought her to the attention of scholars with whom she discussed theology.

According to Smith's account, the Chesapeake warriors took him to Powhatan, who demanded to know what the Englishman was doing in his territory. Unsatisfied with's Smith's answer, the sachem ordered him put to death by having his head clubbed against a rock. Before this could happen, however, Powhatan's daughter Pocahontas rushed forward and threw herself across Smith's body, begging for his life. Powhatan could deny his favorite daughter nothing, and set Smith free. Thereafter the Indian girl and the English adventurer were the best of friends.

This romantic account did more than all of Smith's real accomplishments to win him immortality, but it leads to too many questions. Smith's own evidence is contradictory. He makes it appear, in this account, as if he met Powhatan for the first time when he was brought before the sachem as a captive. Actually he had been dealing with Powhatan long before he was taken captive by the Chesapeakes. Nor does he explain why the Chesapeakes, the enemies of Powhatan's confederation, should have handed a prize captive to the chief of their foes. Nor is there any reason why Powhatan, who had been bartering amicably with Smith for many months, should suddenly take offense at the Englishman's presence in his domain.

Even if the story were true, however—and there is a ring of truth to some aspects of it—it is not as odd or as romantic as it first sounds. Captives were not infrequently saved from death in similar ways. Tribal clans were often depleted by warfare. Women, the heads of the clans, lost husbands, brothers, and sons. It was therefore the right of the leading women of a clan to rescue a promising captive from death. The captive was then adopted into the clan of his rescuer, becoming, in effect, the replacement for a male killed in war. He was considered and treated as part of his new tribe from that time on. Pocahontas was certainly one of the highest ranking women of her tribe, and it would not be surprising if she had claimed this right. What would have been both brave and uncharacteristic behavior for a European princess was not at all surprising for Pocahontas, the Indian.

What is more likely, however, is that Smith did not meet Pocahontas until she was a grown woman. Whether or not he met her during her visits to the Jamestown colony is a question that cannot be answered. It was in Jamestown that she met and married John Rolfe, a widower with two small children who had come to the colony after it was well established to grow tobacco. But considering her social success in London, it would have been out of character for Smith, whether or not he already knew her, not to claim some sort of prior acquaintance. Naturally, his claim was spectacular.

Seventeenth-century writers further embellished the tale by claiming that Smith was responsible for Pocahontas's conversion to Christianity, over the objections of her family. Her family may have found it strange, but they did not object to her conversion or to her marriage, and Smith could not rightfully claim any credit. The Reverend Thomas Fuller, author of *The Worthies of England*, a book published in the 1660s, indignantly called Smith a liar, but his charge was ignored. Fact or fiction, the legend of the brave captain saved by the Indian princess was too good to forget, and it became part of folklore.

Even the end of the story is suspicious, smacking of Smith's overripe imagination. This ending is not even hinted at in the footnotes to the 1616 edition of *A True Relation*, but is described in detail in the *Generall Historie* of 1624. Powhatan only agreed to set Smith free on condition that the Chickahominy be given two cannon and a millstone. Warriors went with him to be sure the conditions were met.

When Smith and his escort arrived at Jamestown, the settlers were overjoyed to see him, having given him up for dead. When he explained the conditions attached to his release, the colonists took two demiculverins, enormous cannon usually mounted on warships, and filled them with stones. When they were fired, the stones crashed into the forest, knocking down several large trees and completely terrifying the warriors. The braves then tried to lift the cannon, were unable to do so, and were just as happy to leave without them.

It is hard to imagine that Smith, a competent military leader ever mindful of the colony's safety, would have made such a promise. Even if he had promised, under duress, he would not have considered keeping his word. Furthermore, demiculverins were enormous artillery pieces, weighing between four and five thousand pounds apiece, made of iron and brass. They were capable of firing a nine-pound shot about one thousand yards. The two at Jamestown had been brought ashore with great difficulty. The special hoists for them broke twice, and one fell into the James River (it was only recovered after many days of hard labor). If an incident such as he had described had taken place, and had a demonstration been made for the benefit of the Chickahominy warriors, mention would have been made of it in other chronicles. No one else writing about the early years of Jamestown even touches on the subject, so it is reasonable to assume that the incident was merely another product of Smith's imagination.

 **16**

H owever Smith achieved his freedom, he returned to Jamestown on January 7, 1608. The colony, as usual, was in ferment. Gabriel Archer had talked Ratcliffe into giving him a seat on the council, over the objections of John Martin. Archer had persuaded Ratcliffe that they should make an official voyage to England soon. Apparently life in the New World was too much for them.

Smith immediately declared that he would use every firearm in the settlement, including the cannon, to prevent the sailing. Archer, who had thought Smith safely dead in the interior, knew he had a problem. He promptly charged Smith with the responsibility for the loss of two of his men to the Indians.

The following morning Smith's "trial" took place. Why Archer bothered with even this mockery of justice is unclear, for in less than an hour Smith had been found guilty. He was sentenced to be hanged at dawn the next day.

Ratcliffe and Archer supposed they would then be free to leave for England, but their scheme collapsed that same afternoon. A ship was sighted sailing up the James: it was Captain Newport in the *Susan Constant*. His sister ship, the *Phoenix*, commanded by Captain Francis Nelson, had been lost in a storm, but Newport had pressed on. He had left England six weeks earlier, and he arrived in the proverbial nick of time to save Smith's life.

Wingfield, who was to have been executed with Smith, was also set free, and Archer and Ratcliffe were forbidden to leave the colony. Newport then proceeded to take stock of the settlement.

Of the original 105 settlers, 38 remained. There was a serious shortage of gunpowder and ammunition, and of course such things as English clothing and lamp oil.

Newport had brought provisions of almost every kind. The *Susan Constant*'s hold was filled with munitions, tools, clothing, blankets, and food. Even more important were the eighty new recruits for the settlement.

Smith, restored to his council position by Newport, put everyone to work. New houses had to be built, and the skeleton of a new and permanent church was constructed. Smith felt that the Reverend Mr. Hunt should have a suitable structure in which to deliver his sermons.

The new building program received a drastic setback in less than a week. A fire broke out in one of the thatched-roof houses and spread rapidly. Before it could be put out it had destroyed a dozen houses and a section of the fort. Many men lost all their clothes and possessions. Worst off was the Reverend Hunt, who had lost all the books in his precious library. He nevertheless held a thanksgiving service in gratitude that no lives had been lost. Smith immediately had men begin repair work on the fort, stopping all other construction to do so.

While Smith was thus engaged, Archer resumed scheming behind his back. He was anxious to prove to Newport that Smith was not the only one capable of dealing with the Indians. He hoped that by impressing Newport he could win a permanent position from the directors in London. Archer therefore made a journey into the interior, returning with quantities of food. The good impression he sought faded, however, when it was learned that he had paid four times as much as Smith was accustomed to paying.

Archer was not the only one to set about spoiling the market. The members of Newport's crew were eager for souvenirs and curiosities to take back to England with them. In defiance of Smith's orders, they sneaked off to the Indian villages to do their own trading. The Indians soon learned that the market had improved, and Smith complained to Newport that goods for which he had formerly paid a penny's worth in trinkets now cost him a pound's worth.

Three gentlemen were among the new settlers to the colony. They were Matthew Scrivener and William and Michael Phettiplace. Scrivener, a thin, quiet young man, had been given a place on the council by the London directors. Archer and Ratcliffe were contemptuous of his reserve, but Smith believed himself a better judge of character. He thought Scrivener was dependable and honest, and was impressed by his marksmanship and swordsmanship. Scrivener became one of Smith's lieutenants.

Newport and Scrivener accompanied Smith on several trips to the Indian villages and were impressed with his ability to get along with the natives. Although the villagers ran from the unfamiliar Englishmen, they soon reappeared at the sight of Smith's familiar figure and seemed genuinely glad to see him. Newport was able to go on many such trips, for he was unable to sail until spring. Fox and other fur-bearing animals were hard to find, so it was not possible to fill the fur quota in winter. Nor could the men work long in the forests cutting trees for lumber; it was too cold.

By the tenth of April, however, the hold was filled. And by that time most of the provisions Newport had brought from England had been consumed, and the colony was again low on food supplies. The *Phoenix*, on which they had been depending, still had not arrived, and was presumed to be lost.

Wingfield was being sent back to England at the insistence of the whole council. Smith suggested that Archer go, too, and Archer went. Now that he was secure, Smith was not vindictive against his former enemies, and pushed a motion through the council dropping all charges against them. He did not wish to harm their futures.

Ratcliffe should have taken passage back to England with them, but he had determined to remain the colony's president. Only a day after the sailing of the *Susan Constant* he blew off his hand while cleaning his musket. The doctor saved his life, but he was afterwards a weak, sick, and shaken man. The colony's government fell on Smith's shoulders.

The situation was not helped by the colonists' continuous dream of gold. The directors in London had persisted in disseminating false information, and many of the colonists were only too ready to believe in the availability of precious metals. It would be much easier, they thought, to go treasure hunting than to work in the fields growing corn and vegetables.

The men took action on their dreams on the morning of April 12. Smith found himself faced with a group of

95

rebellious settlers, refusing to do the scheduled work assigned them. Instead, they said, they were going gold hunting. The men were all newly arrived settlers. The veteran colonists knew better than to engage in such foolishness and went off to their assigned tasks. Smith, not one for subtlety, loaded his pistols in full view of the now apprehensive men, and shoved them into his belt.

Smith then made a speech. He could jail the ringleaders for mutiny, he told the new settlers, but he would not. He could even execute those who refused to work, but he would not. If they wanted to look for gold, they could look for gold. If they wanted to spend all their time looking for gold, he would not stop them.

The delighted immigrants, thinking the speech was over, started to cheer, but Smith quickly silenced them. Jamestown, he continued, existed under a royal patent. Only those who accepted a share of responsibility in the community's problems could expect the protection of the town's arms, or the right to share in the food in the warehouses. The gold-seekers were free to leave, but not free to return. They could go anywhere they wished on the North American continent, but they could not return to Jamestown unless they were willing to work for the community.

The settlers listened to his speech. Then they thought about it for a while in silence. The ringleaders were the first to collect their hoes and spades, and the others soon followed. That was the end of the great Jamestown gold hunt.

 **17**

J UST after dawn on the morning of
April 20 the sentry on duty fired a pistol. This was the
agreed warning of danger to the settlement. A few mo-
ments later all colonists were awakened by the trum-
peter, and they scurried to their assigned places in the
fort, dressing and arming as they went.

When Smith arrived he saw, through his spyglass, a
large ship in the distance. Although Ratcliffe was still
very sick, it was felt that his expertise was needed, and
he was brought from his bed. Ratcliffe thought the vessel
was a Spanish warship that had discovered the colony
and intended to attack.

Smith disagreed with the sick president, saying that
the ship looked more like a merchantman. No one was
willing to take chances, however, and the cannon were
readied and the muskets loaded. Most of the new immigrants, who had had no military training, huddled at the
rear of the fort.

In less than an hour the ship was clearly visible and
broke out her pennant: the British flag. It was the *Phoenix*, sailing up the James River to the town's new wharf.

Captain Francis Nelson, master of the *Phoenix*, had
survived the storms at sea and made it to port. His arrival

was the miracle the colony needed. All his cargo was intact; he and his passengers and crew had lived on food bartered from West Indian natives. Even better, his decks were filled with the large haul of "tunny" fish they had caught the previous day.

The *Phoenix* received a warm welcome, and everyone, even the forty new settlers she had brought, went to work salting the tuna to preserve it. The community now numbered 158 men and boys, not counting the ship's crew, but there was more than enough for everyone to eat.

As the weather improved, so did the spirits of the settlers. Where before men had been able to think only of getting back to England, a new optimism prevailed. Smith put everyone to work. Trees were cut, stumps pulled, farmlands enlarged and cleared, houses built. The new settlers spent at least two hours each day learning to handle firearms.

There was good reason for the military precautions. The Chesapeake had been stealing tools left out by careless settlers. Even some of Powhatan's Chickahominy had been causing trouble, as it became obvious to some of Powhatan's under-sachems that the English were not only there to stay, but there to expand.

Smith knew that the offenses would continue unless he took definite action. He set out with twenty men to try to capture the thieves. He caught five Chickahominy and took them back to Jamestown with him. There he tied them to the mainmast of the *Phoenix*, threatened them with torture, and shot off muskets only a few inches from their faces. He then released them to return to their own villages. For a while that was the end of problems from the Chickahominy.

Smith spent all his spare time during this period writing his first book, *A True Relation*. He sat up late into the night working, in the new large house into which he had recently moved with Martin and Scrivener. He exaggerated only minimally in *A True Relation*. His main purpose was to give readers in England an accurate representation of New World conditions and to give a factual history of the colony. It annoyed him that settlers still arrived filled with a desire for gold and easy riches, and he wanted the public to know the truth. The truth, he believed, would bring a different class of immigrant to Jamestown, one better able to withstand the hardships of the early colony.

Smith wrote relatively modestly of his own achievements, and he was so loyal to the colony, for which he felt so much responsibility, that he minimized even the bitter feuds and dissension that had threatened to destroy the settlement. The accuracy of *A True Relation* makes it Smith's best book. Its quiet statement of facts carries more authority than his later flamboyance.

Smith also wrote a number of long and detailed reports for geographer Hakluyt. He enclosed maps and charts that he had drawn himself, and he also included a series of maps of the American coastline for Henry Hudson. He based the maps for Hudson on information he had gained from Bartholomew Gosnold before he died.

Smith's energy was remarkable. As well as finding the time to write, he was in charge of daily administration of the colony. He supervised the military training of newcomers and kept close watch on the grain and vegetable crops so important to the settlement's future. He even took charge of the preparation of a cargo of prime cedar to be sent via the *Phoenix* to the directors in London. He personally selected the trees to be felled, and supervised the making of the planks. Sometimes, though, he misjudged. The height of the New World trees was unusual, and planks often had to be shortened before they could fit into the ship's hold.

Smith also supervised the construction of a new shallop. It weighed about three tons and was very clumsy, being built more like a barge than a sailing ship. It had high sides to withstand rough weather and was considered a practical vessel for any waters more turbulent than those of the James River.

Despite all his duties, Smith's real love was still exploration. He was an adventurer at heart, and he had made up his mind to explore all of Chesapeake Bay.

In late May he completed the manuscript of *A True Relation*, each day adding a few paragraphs to keep it up to date. On June 2 Nelson was ready to sail for England, taking with him Martin, who was in poor health and had to return home. Smith gave Martin his precious manuscript, which he was prepared to pay to have published, a common practice of the times. Once in London, however, Martin proved to be a good literary agent. He persuaded the Prince of Wales to assume financial responsibility for publication of the book, which he hoped would encourage emigration to Virginia.

Smith sailed in the shallop on June 2, accompanying the *Phoenix* as far as Cape Henry, then turning north into Chesapeake Bay. Thirteen men went with Smith. Six were gentlemen-adventurers new to Jamestown who had no idea of the hardships the journey might entail. One was a blacksmith with no qualifications other than physical strength. And there were two veteran colonists, three former soldiers, and a doctor, whose services they hoped would be unnecessary.

It was primarily this voyage, combined with a later trip Smith made on the Bay, that enabled him to draw an accurate map of the region. He even sketched in the location of Indian villages, information that would be very important to future settlers. This map, along with Smith's detailed description of the region, was published in 1612. It alone would have assured him an important place among New World explorers. He made a few minor mistakes, but he performed his task with no instruments other than a compass. Considering what he had to work with, his results are all the more astonishing.

Smith's research was thorough. He never rushed, taking care to sketch each curve of the shoreline. Chickahominy-speaking Accowmack Indians helped him, and they described nearby tribes for him. Smith enjoyed himself immensely.

The others did not. The shallop was an open boat, and the men were drenched by frequent rainstorms. Heavy winds twice broke the masts, and they had to go ashore to repair them. By mid-June the gentlemen were thoroughly sick of the adventure and wanted nothing more than to return to Jamestown.

Smith would not abandon the voyage. They had a month's supply of food and he would not turn back until that, at least, was depleted. He had no sympathy for the exhaustion of his men. Besides, both men and rain-soaked bread would dry quickly in the sun.

Smith discovered the mouth of the Potomac River on June 16. The discovery lifted everyone's spirits, and the company decided immediately to sail upstream. It was obvious that the river was a major waterway, and the crew was excited. They sailed upstream for more than thirty miles before a band of warriors appeared, making threatening gestures on one of the banks. Smith ordered muskets fired, and the braves left.

Smith did think it diplomatic, however, to visit the nearby village and speak with the local sachem. He eyed the rich soil thoughtfully, thinking of future settlements, and he was equally impressed by the abundance of beaver, sable, and otter furs. The river teemed with so many fish that the physician, Walter Russell, tried to scoop some of them up with his frying pan, hoping to save himself a step in cooking. He did not succeed.

A few days later Smith tried another method of fishing: spearing the fish with his sword. This soon became great sport for all the crew, and they had more than enough fish for everyone. On the following day Smith tried again but met with a misfortune. Anas Todkill, whose narrative was published in Smith's *A Map of Virginia*, describes what happened:

It chanced the captaine taking a fish from his sword (not knowing her condition) being much the fashion of a Thornebacke with a longer taile, whereon is a most poysoned sting of 2 or 3 inches long, which she strooke an inche and halfe into the wrist of his arme the which in 4 houres had so extreamly swolne his hand, arme, shoulder, and part of his body, as we al with much sorrow concluded his funerall, and prepared his grave in an Ile hard by (as himselfe appointed) which then wee called stingeray Ile after the name of the fish.

Smith suffered excruciating pain. The crew heaved to among the shoals, expecting him to die. Everyone was in deepest gloom. All ended well, however, as Todkill explains.

Yet by the helpe of a precious oile Doctour Russel applyed ere night his tormenting paine was so wel asswaged that he eate the fish to his supper, which gave no less joy and content to us, then ease to himselfe.

Unfortunately, a more serious accident incapacitated Todkill, when he tripped over a rock and broke his leg. Russell could not give the man the attention he needed on the shallop, so Smith decided to return to Jamestown.

When they reached Jamestown on July 21 they found the settlement in chaos. They had been gone for only seven weeks. Many of the newly-arrived settlers had become ill from the heat of the Virginia swamplands in summer. Others were furious because Ratcliffe, still president, had diverted them from their regular work and was insisting that they build him a fine house.

No sooner had Smith come ashore than he was approached by a deputation of gentlemen and commoners alike, unanimously demanding that Ratcliffe resign and Smith replace him. Surprisingly, Smith was upset. However much he may have wanted the post, he was convinced that a president must serve out his full term. The community had to develop a thorough respect for authority, which could not happen if the president of the settlement was forced to rely on the goodwill of a mob to retain his office.

No one else agreed with him. They wanted Smith for president, and only Smith, and he could not sway them. Ratcliffe, still sick, and aware of the sentiment against him, solved the problem by resigning. On July 21, the day he returned to Jamestown, Smith was unanimously elected president of the colony.

Smith insisted that he be allowed to appoint his own

deputy, who would become acting president whenever Smith left the colony. He also insisted that he be given a free hand in selecting staff members whom he believed to be honest and competent. The colonists and the council agreed to these stipulations. Smith immediately named Matthew Scrivener as his deputy.

Now that Smith had the presidency, a post he had always wanted, he could not wait to leave the settlement. He was far more interested in adventure and the excitement of journeys of exploration than he was in attending to his administrative duties. He had become tired of administration when he was president in everything but name. He was also certain that Jamestown would be in good hands with Scrivener directing its affairs. He spent only three days at the settlement before setting out again in the shallop. Nine members of his original crew, five gentlemen and four commoners, were anxious to go with him, and volunteers made up the rest of the party.

Smith immediately sailed north again to the mouth of the Potomac. One evening six of his men became ill after eating a strange kind of fish, and Smith decided they had better spend the night on board the shallop. They anchored a short distance away from the shore of Chesapeake Bay.

It was just as well that they took precautions that night. Early the next morning the sentry reported that eight large war canoes, filled with Indian warriors, were approaching the shallop. The Indians were heavily armed and seemed intent on making trouble. Smith could see bows, arrows, knives, and spears glinting from a distance.

Smith knew he did not have enough force to respond to the threat; he had to rely on trickery. He was certain he would be attacked and overwhelmed if he showed his weakness. The men who had been suffering from indigestion were still sick, so Smith ordered them hidden beneath the tarpaulins. The other members of the company collected all the hats and helmets they could find on board. These they propped on top of tall sticks and swords, so that only their tops showed above the high sides of the shallop. When the warriors approached near enough to see the boat more closely, they thought a large party was on board. Completely taken in by Smith's ruse, they withdrew.

After several more days the colonists reached the northern end of Chesapeake Bay. There Smith discovered the mouth of another large river. He met some friendly Indians on the shores, who gave him a warning: a tall, husky tribe known as the Susquehannocks lived on the river. They permitted no one to travel upstream without their permission. Smith offered to pay his informants to go to the Susquehannock as messengers to say that he came as a friend, with gifts. They accepted.

Smith waited two days before a band of about sixty warriors appeared. They also brought gifts, including quarters of venison that were greatly appreciated by the explorers. They spoke a Chickahominy dialect, which enabled Smith to understand them, and he spent a long time discussing the course of the river. He was still hopeful that this might prove to be the sought-for passage to the Pacific. Although finally convinced that it was not a waterway between the two oceans, he was still curious enough to spend three days traveling upstream in the company of the warriors. The new river that he discovered, explored, and mapped, was the Susquehanna.

At the end of the three days he was deep in the wilder-

105

ness of the region that would become Pennsylvania. The English and the Susquehannock exchanged more gifts, and Smith promised them he would return the next year to trade with them. He then turned the shallop around and started back toward Jamestown.

As he sailed south through the Bay he continued mapping. He crossed over to the western side to make a short journey up the Patuxent River, the one large river in the area that he had not yet explored or mapped. He soon realized that it was a relatively small stream, and started the journey back to the Bay.

There were unfortunate consequences from this trip, however. Members of Smith's company had been eager, in varying degrees, to try out different New World foods. One gentleman-adventurer, Richard Fetherstone, ate some strange berries he found growing near the shore, and became desperately ill. Anthony Bagnall, the doctor currently accompanying the small exploration party, did his best to save him, but within an hour Fetherstone was dead. The company was horror-stricken, and they buried him with full military honors.

Many thought it was time to end the voyage, and Smith, for all practical purposes, agreed. Nevertheless, there was one more thing he wanted to do before returning to Jamestown: thoroughly explore the southern shore of the Bay. This may have seemed like a good idea, but the territory unfortunately belonged to the Chesapeake, the enemies of the colonists and their ally, Powhatan.

Smith sailed fifteen miles up the Elizabeth River before he turned back, and he undoubtedly set foot on what was to be the site of the future town of Norfolk. There he made an unexpected discovery. The area was inhabited by the small tribe of the Nansemond, which owed allegiance to neither Powhatan's confederation nor the Chesapeake. They presented him with gifts: four hundred large baskets of corn and, as Smith wrote in *A Map of Virginia*, "so many bales of dried venison that the shallop sat low in the water." He established lasting relations with this tribe.

Smith had gathered an enormous store of knowledge and information on this trip. It was to prove immensely valuable later, both to planners of colonial ventures in England, who needed to know the best areas for planting settlements, and to those who would do the actual colonizing and needed to know every detail of an otherwise unknown territory. Smith's mission was an even greater success in immediate terms. He was returning to Jamestown with large supplies of grain and meat, enough to feed those in the settlement for many days. Although he greatly enjoyed his journey of exploration, it was not a holiday from responsibility. He remembered that he was president of Jamestown.

 18

In the late morning of September 7, 1608, Matthew Scrivener and a welcoming party went down to the wharf to greet the explorers as soon as the shallop was seen approaching shore. Smith went ashore prepared to face a new host of problems that would need immediate attention. He was ready for the worst, as problems always seemed to arise while he was gone.

He was pleasantly surprised. The affairs of the settlement were much less chaotic than they had been in the past after Smith's absences. Scrivener was a good deputy, a reliable and efficient manager during the absence of the president. But he was still new to the colony and to conditions in a frontier society. He had hesitated to make decisions in some matters if he was unfamiliar with all of the circumstances. Smith had no time to rest from his journey, but bent all of his energies to administrative work.

Unfortunately, the first and most important matter was a personal problem, probably one with which Smith would rather not have dealt. Ratcliffe, the former president, had been charged in Smith's absence with mutiny, conspiracy, and treason. The charges were greatly exaggerated, and Ratcliffe had been imprisoned—which probably saved his life. Scrivener had to take a firm stand and post guards to prevent enraged colonists from breaking into the cell at the fort and lynching Ratcliffe. Hard times made feelings in the tiny colony run high.

Smith immediately reviewed all the evidence and found it much exaggerated. He set Ratcliffe free and issued a firm proclamation to the settlers announcing that he would himself prosecute anyone who tried to harm Ratcliffe. The former president, he said, was still a sick man, not yet recovered from his accident.

Jamestown began to flourish, for the first time, under Smith's administration. New work schedules were drawn up for everyone. Construction was begun on solid new houses for the next batch of immigrants, who were expected at almost any time. New warehouses were built, in expectation of a surplus of supplies, and streets were laid out in an orderly fashion. The summer had been damp, so damp that many roofs had rotted. All that needed it were replaced, and construction was also resumed on Ratcliffe's "palace," which Smith was going to convert into a meeting hall.

Settlers were encouraged to make products themselves, such as woodcarvings, and to sell them in a new small shop located a short distance from the new church. A higher second wall was built around the town for better defense, and land was cleared far beyond the planted fields, so that anyone approaching the settlement could be seen from a distance.

Smith was not satisfied with the fort itself. From what he knew about the Indians' methods of surprise attacks, he decided that the triangular shape of the fort was inadequate. He gave the matter considerable thought and concluded that a star-shaped, five-pointed fort would better suit their needs. In that way flank support could be given with muskets to any portion of the building under attack.

He sketched his idea on paper, and the already over-worked colonists began enlarging and changing the shape of the fort. It was all done under Scrivener's careful direction. So successful did Smith's design prove that it later became standard throughout the British colonies from New England to Georgia. It was used until the time of the Revolution, over a century and a half later.

Each evening Smith dined privately with Scrivener and his small staff of assistants. They reviewed the accomplishments of the day, outlined future plans, and revised where revision was needed.

Military training had fallen off during the greatest heat of the summer months. Now everyone was ordered to resume drilling, musket practice, and wilderness skirmishing. Every Sunday after worship services formal drills were held in a clearing beyond the town's palisades, which became known as Smith Field. Smith's little army was not very impressive by European standards, but it was a novelty that never failed to amaze Indian visitors who stopped to watch. The firearms, of course, were the main attraction, and Smith made sure, whenever there were Indian guests, that the men fired at targets large enough to hit.

The food situation was better than it had been since the founding of the colony. Some of the corn crop had been spoiled by rain and the all-pervasive dampness, but planting had been extensive, in preparation for any contingency. The harvest was ample, so much so that the storehouse overflowed and it was necessary to construct an addition. Smith had new fields cleared for grain and

110

vegetables, but he had been turned down once by the council on the question of growing tobacco and he did not make the suggestion again.

The settlers worked so hard that they were exhausted by the end of the day. They went to bed soon after supper, having little energy for any form of recreation. Smith did not join them, however. When his other activities were over for the day, Smith sat down to another project: working alone on his new book.

A Map of Virginia, with a Description of the Country, was written with posterity in mind. *A True Relation* had been written with a desire to clear up prevalent misconceptions about the New World and to tell people the truth about the colony at Jamestown, but Smith hoped that *A Map of Virginia* would win him lasting fame. It did. He labored hard every night, for he wanted to put his impressions on paper while they were still fresh to him, and he carefully checked his sketches and notes to make sure there were no mistakes in the manuscript.

His own great experience as a traveler and an explorer, combined with his training under Hakluyt and Plancius, had made him an excellent mapmaker. He knew the advantages of accurately portraying a strange new land, and he took great care with his maps and charts, knowing how valuable they would be to others.

A Map of Virginia was a masterpiece of cartography, and Smith knew it would assure him a place in history. Perhaps it was this knowledge that caused him to indulge in a piece of vanity that injured his reputation. He was unable to resist inserting a pen-and-ink sketch of himself on the major map in the book. The critics of his own time naturally attacked such egotism, but in time this gesture of self-love was forgiven. Simon van der

Paas, an artist who was Smith's contemporary, used this sketch as a basis for the portrait he drew. Unfortunately there is no way of judging its accuracy, as its foundation is Smith's own conception of himself.

Smith noted in his new book that twenty-eight colonists had died during the summer, succumbing to the heat. The settlement was situated among tidewater swamps, which were not considered healthful. Smith noticed, however, that the veteran colonists did not become ill as easily as the new arrivals. He concluded that the longer a man remained in the New World the more acclimated he became, and the less susceptible to unfamiliar sicknesses and hardships. This is a very reasonable assumption, and the Pilgrims, when they settled New England a decade later, were to make the same discovery. The longer a man survived, the greater were his chances of continuing to do so.

Five weeks after Smith returned to Jamestown, in mid-October, the *Susan Constant* returned for the third time, bringing much needed supplies and food. Captain Newport was in charge, and this time he brought with him seventy immigrants. The directors in London gave places on the council to two new gentleman-adventurers, Richard Waldo and Peter Winne. Both were hardworking and competent, and proved their worth to the colony.

Two of the new immigrants had a far more drastic effect on the settlement than all of the previous arrivals. The first women had arrived at Jamestown, ending the days of the all-male settlement. Smith immediately prohibited gambling, brawling, and cursing in public. The men were also directed to make use of the outhouses instead of open clearings, and they no longer stripped to the minimum in hot weather. Men were much more careful of their appearance, and trimmed their beards and even changed their clothes more frequently.

Very little is known about the women who brought about such changes. One was Mistress Forest, who may have been the wife of Thomas Forest, a gentleman-adventurer, or perhaps the wife of George Forest, who may have been related to Thomas. Nothing more is known of her.

The other woman was her maidservant, Anne Burrowes, a young woman in her early twenties. In *A Map of Virginia* Smith described her as "lively, intelligent and modest." She must have greatly enlivened the spirits of the colony. About a year after she arrived she married John Laydon, a member of the original expedition. The ceremony was performed by the Reverend Hunt. Laydon had begun as a laborer but had become an expert farmer by the time he married. The Laydons were the first couple to marry and rear a family in the New World. Their sons were small plantation owners but their grandsons became wealthy tobacco growers. The Laydons were thus founders of early American aristocracy.

The presence of the women had an even greater symbolic than practical significance to the settlers. Jamestown was now considered a permanent settlement, and other men began to think of bringing their wives or sweethearts to the new land. Smith suggested, urged by some of the men, that the directors of the London Company send out ships with unattached female immigrants. Many of the colonists were thinking of settling down and making the land truly their own.

Newport had also brought with him a number of for-

113

eigners, some Dutch and some Polish, suddenly trans-
forming Jamestown into a multilingual community. The
presence of these immigrants would later cause frictions,
but Smith had no time to plan ahead for that eventuality.
Newport carried directives from the investors concerning the foreigners that Smith felt would be impossible to
carry out.

Smith was told that the Dutch and Poles were to be
put to work in a factory making glass and tar, products
for which there was considerable demand in England.
The investors thought they saw a chance to increase
their profits, but Smith knew that every immigrant had
to work in the fields and must hunt and fish to assure the
colony's survival. Jamestown was not yet well enough
established to support an artisan community.

This was not all. The directors had refused to believe
Smith's account in *A True Relation,* or even to accept
Newport's eyewitness descriptions of the land around
the colony. They were still convinced that the country
was rich with veins of gold and mines of precious gems.
Newport was ordered not to return to England without
a large supply of both items.

Newport had been angry, but the long sea voyage had
calmed him. Smith was less philosophical; he was furious. He cursed so violently that the staid Scrivener became upset. Smith had hoped that the colony's supporters had been given some idea of the hardships and of
Jamestown's continual struggle to become self-sustain-
ing. It was obvious that the directors had no such idea,
nor did they understand that there simply were no mines
of jewels or gold in the area.

The worst was still to come. The president of the
colony was ordered to hold a coronation ceremony for

Powhatan, and give the sachem a gold crown. In return, they were to receive from the chief a pledge of his allegiance to King James. The idea should have been laughable, but Smith was livid. He had an idea of how Powhatan might receive such an offer, if it were thoroughly explained to him.

That, suggested Newport, was exactly what they should not do. Rather than explain the situation to Powhatan, they should simply go through the motions of obeying the orders for the benefit of the directors in London. The two men therefore paid a visit to Powhatan, bringing the gifts that had been sent him from London.

Powhatan had no use for the gilded crown, which he politely accepted, but the scarlet, silk-lined cape he understood and enjoyed. The other personal gift from Powhatan's "brother monarch" was confusing to a man who slept on a fur-covered platform. It was a huge four-poster bed, complete with a feather-stuffed mattress, the first of its kind in North America. No one knows what Powhatan thought of it, nor what became of it: the bed vanished soon after it was presented. Almost certainly it was not used for the purpose for which it had been intended.

Powhatan graciously sent two beaver pelts and a fine lynx hide to King James. He pretended not to hear, however, when Smith, in spite of his prearranged decision, attempted to explain that the sachem was to acknowledge James as his overlord. Smith quickly gave up the attempt, realizing that if he pressed farther he might make an enemy of the most powerful chief in the region. Powhatan had no reason to humble himself to a man he had never seen. Both Smith and Newport mentioned the incident in their reports, and that was that.

Smith needed all the time he had to help the new immigrants adjust to the primitive living conditions that still prevailed in the colony, but he was forced to use some of it in what he knew would be a fruitless search for gold. Accompanied by Newport and a small group of men, Smith sailed up the James River in the shallop. When they came to the falls in the river, Smith and his party left the shallop under guard and marched inland on foot.

They marched forty miles inland but found only Indian villages, no native gold mines. One member of the party, a metal refiner by the name of William Callicut, declared that he had found a small deposit of silver in the ground. Smith was convinced it was worthless, but the man took samples anyway.

When the expedition returned to Jamestown, Smith and Newport prepared reports for the directors. Smith put his overdeveloped imagination to good use in this report. His single shallop was magically transformed into a large flotilla of ships and his brief overland march into an enormous search conducted by brave men who fanned out in a wide hunt through savage terrain.

After his report was concluded, Smith went back to the real work that had been waiting for him in Jamestown. He sent Scrivener off to barter for corn with the Indians, and he sent messengers ahead to the local sachems telling them of the valuable items he had to trade: knives, mirrors, and blankets. He indicated that he wanted furs in exchange for these goods, and the chiefs were happy to comply.

Smith's greatest task was the indoctrination of the immigrants. Some of the newcomers found it hard to adapt to the colony's ways, and Smith had to take their education in hand.

A typical case was that of two newly arrived gentlemen, Gabriel Beadle and John Russell. They were both London playboys who had come to the New World for the fun of it. They had never worked in their lives, and they had no intention of starting now. Smith, on the other hand, was determined that they earn their way.

The two young men were put to work in the forest near the settlement, chopping down some of the enormous trees that grew there. Neither gentleman had seen a tree of that height in England, much less thought of cutting one down. Their hands rapidly became blistered, a matter they sought to relieve by cursing.

Smith had not forgotten his prohibitions against profanity. A member of his staff recorded every curse, and Beadle and Russell were brought before the entire community. For every transgression they had a can of water poured up their sleeves. Much later the two cold, drenched gentlemen were released. Thereafter they chopped trees in silence.

A week later their hands had toughened and they were mastering the skill of chopping trees. They were, allegedly, able to accomplish more in an hour than they had originally been able to do in a day. Eventually they became pillars of the community, conscientious men who "learned to look with loathing upon their former noxious pastimes," as Smith remarked in *A Map of Virginia.*

There were other problems. The orders of the London directors could not be completely ignored. Even though the Dutch and Polish arrivals were desperately needed

117

to work in the fields or help with the other tasks of the community, Smith put them to work making glass and tar. The entire population of the settlement had to stop work briefly to help them out, and the finished products were loaded into the hold of the *Susan Constant*.

Scrivener made the rounds of the Indian towns but returned with only small quantities of grain. Although the Indians usually had large stores on hand, the colonists were beginning to drain even their resources. Consequently Smith had to take time he could little afford from his other duties to visit some of the Indian villages himself. The Indians were always more willing to trade with him. He was so successful that Ratcliffe, forgetting his obligations to Smith in a wave of envy, asked Newport to depose the president.

Newport, naturally, had no such idea in mind, nor did he have the necessary authority to depose Smith even if he had wanted to. At that point relations between Smith and Newport were becoming strained because of a situation neither was able to control. The sailors of Newport's crew were unable to refrain from breaking the laws of Jamestown, and even defied the instructions of the London directors by trading with the Indians for furs. The pelts would bring high prices in London, and they did not hesitate to barter butter, oatmeal, pickled beef, and even beer for what they wanted.

The colonists' market was rapidly being destroyed, forcing them to pay much more than they were accustomed to for anything they needed from the Indians. Smith complained to Newport, asking that the mariner discipline his crew. Newport, however, was unable to halt the illicit trade, and subsequently tried to come to the defense of his men. Smith let things go as long as he could but eventually lost patience with Newport. He took the matter upon himself and placed three members of the *Susan Constant*'s crew in detention. The sailors took the hint and ceased their illicit trade with the Indians, but Smith and Newport rarely spoke to one another. It was an unfortunate cooling of relations between the men who were primarily responsible for the continued existence of the colony.

There was a great demand in England for "red roots," or sassafras, which supposedly had powerful medicinal properties. The Indians used all parts of the plant—bark, leaves, roots, and flowers—and the English were quick to catch on. So great was its impression on European medicine that whole shiploads were eventually sent over to the Old World, and it became a major American product and a source of wealth. Sassafras was considered a remedy for everything from coughs and sniffles to the plague and the "French Pox." It has remained important in folk medicine everywhere it grows. Today it is used in root beer and, because of its stimulant and carminative properties, in pharmaceutical preparations as well.

Smith felt it was his duty to obtain for the directors what they wanted. He made a five-day trip into the interior and returned with a supply of sassafras roots from the Indians. This, too, was duly loaded aboard the *Susan Constant*.

In early November 1608 the *Susan Constant* was loaded. Her hold was filled with lumber, glass, and tar, and bales of fur were lashed on the decks, under tarpaulins so they would not rot in the hold. There was enough sassafras on board to delight the hearts of the London doctors. Unfortunately, there was not a single ounce of gold.

Smith knew there was no gold to be found, and he also

knew the directors would be very upset if they did not get any. He and Newport put aside their feud and got together to see what sort of plan they could concoct. They knew they had to work together to save the colony from the consequences of any more foolish orders from London.

Smith wrote a report to the directors, explaining once again that there was no gold, no precious metals. Nonetheless, he sent along a large supply of ore that some of the gold-hunting settlers had brought in. It was the closest thing to gold they had found. This ore was duly shipped to London, where it was found, on analysis, to be iron pyrite, that mineral known today by the popular name "fool's gold."

The riches of the New World did not lie in gold, Smith wrote. He detailed the colony's true situation, its desperate struggle for survival, and its great potential. He enclosed maps that he had drawn of their region of Virginia, and of Chesapeake Bay. He described the land, the navigable rivers, and the disposition of the local Indian tribes. He extolled the rich soil, the mild climate, the vast supplies of timber, and above all the opportunity to create a British empire on the continent.

In a separate package he sent maps to Henry Hudson, who received them before he left England to work for the Dutch. In March 1609, only a few months later, Hudson sailed to the New World with his mixed crew of English and Dutch. He used Smith's maps as a guide to the North American coastline. It was then that he discovered the river that today bears his name.

Much of Smith's letter was devoted to criticizing the type of immigrant London was sending to Jamestown. Most of them were not suited to wilderness living, and

120

many died as a result of hardships they were not able to endure. As if this in itself were not bad enough, they were a definite liability to the colony. Those who did survive gradually became accustomed to frontier life, but they first had to dispense with the foolish dreams of gold and easy wealth they had brought with them from England. The New World needed sturdy people who were willing to work—farmers, fishermen, blacksmiths, masons, "fellows with strong backs and hands who will dig up the root stumps of trees."

The hazards of daily living were increasing, he said. Although the colony now numbered more than two hundred, there was friction between the English and the Poles and the Dutch. Even the Poles and the Dutch, who stood together against the English, quarreled with each other. They could not rely on the Indians for all the food they needed, and a single crop failure could mean disaster for the entire colony. He strongly urged the directors to send at least three ships, preferably four, with badly needed supplies. In this way, he suggested, they would be protecting their investment.

It is unfortunate that the directors did not follow Smith's advice. The colonists had to suffer many more hardships, including the notorious "starving time," before their future became secure.

 **19**

ONE day before the *Susan Constant* left, Smith called a meeting of the council. He urged that Captain Ratcliffe, who could not refrain from troublemaking, be sent back to England. The council was unanimous in its agreement and passed a resolution to that effect. Ratcliffe refused to cooperate, however, insisting that he wanted to remain in Jamestown. Smith was forced to have him escorted to the ship at pistol-point, and he had to station guards along the shore to prevent him from leaving the ship again at the last minute. He might have had help from some of the *Susan Constant*'s crew who would have liked to trade with the natives, but Smith's guards kept the situation under control.

After the ship had sailed, Smith could return to his more usual worries, such as the ever-present food problem. He remembered the promise of the Nansemond to set up permanent trade relations and to supply the colony with a regular delivery of corn and meat. He sent Scrivener with a small party to meet with the Nansemond and take them up on their promise. The men returned disappointed, saying the Indians had changed their minds.

Smith refused to take no for an answer, and he sent Scrivener back with orders to make a show of force. Scrivener went back, and he and his men fired their muskets into the air. The Indians were upset and badly frightened and suddenly eager to trade. They gave Scrivener enough corn to fill three boats.

But the Nansemond were a small tribe and could not meet the increased demand of the expanded colony. Smith was increasingly forced to rely on the Chickahominy. This was a delicate situation. Powhatan had been friendly to the English settlement, but he might not remain so if he knew how much Jamestown had grown and its plans for future expansion. Some of Powhatan's under-sachems, including possibly his own brother, were already eager for the chance to destroy the invaders. Smith would have to proceed very carefully.

Percy, Winne, and Waldo went out on a small food-gathering mission of their own, but had only moderate success. It is possible that many villages were tired of being pressured for food, and the novelty of some of the trade goods had worn off. Also, despite Smith's urging, most colonists refused to learn the native Algonquin dialects and so could not deal easily with the Indians.

By the end of December 1608 the warehouses at Jamestown were emptying rapidly, and the worst of winter was still ahead. Smith knew he had to open negotiations with Powhatan. He asked for slightly less food than the colony needed, hoping to keep Powhatan from guessing the full strength of the colony. He did not invite the sachem to visit the settlement for the same reason, but Powhatan was no fool. He had an idea of what was happening at Jamestown, and he had also discovered that he could set a much higher price for corn than he had previously asked.

The price he asked was that the colonists build him a house. He had in mind as a model the largest building in Jamestown, Ratcliffe's "palace," which had been turned into a meeting hall. In return he would give 150 hogsheads of corn. Smith had no choice but to accept the terms.

Smith himself took charge of the party of forty men that went to Paspahegh to build the house. Scrivener remained behind, under instructions to do his usual competent job as deputy in the absence of the president.

The result was unfortunate. Scrivener had become power hungry, and while Smith was away he schemed behind his back. It would appear that Scrivener had been given enough responsibility to become sure of himself and to think that he alone could handle the duties of the president. The veteran colonists wanted no part of his plan, but some of the recently arrived gentlemen were willing to join him. Fresh from England, they were annoyed by regulations that compelled everyone to work, and they did not yet see the necessity of the rules.

The weather was damp and chill, and the men building the house were greatly hampered by frost and snow. Smith set the example by working twelve hours each day, anxious to get the chore over and done. On Christmas eve he went hunting alone in the forest and shot two wild boar, which were roasted for the workmen's Christmas dinner. They also ate oysters, a number of wildfowl, and baked fish as they enjoyed a whole day off, a pleasant interlude in an unpleasant and difficult job.

The next day the work began again. Smith, who was never lenient, drove the men hard. It is possible that he drove them too hard, because several became unhappy. A plot was initiated among the Dutch carpenters to murder Smith, and several of the English colonists went along with it. Eventually they decided that it would be too risky for them to do the actual killing, and that it would be better for everyone if they could somehow persuade the Indians to do it for them.

Some of the original Jamestown settlers were part of the group, however, and their respect for Smith was too great to go along with the plan. One of them went to Smith secretly, telling him of the plot. Smith reacted typically. He did not take the warning seriously and contemptuously brushed aside all mention of rebellion. It is possible that he considered it merely the grumbling of overworked men.

For a while it seemed as if he were right. Work continued, and no one made a hostile gesture. On the surface all was calm, but the workers had been active behind Smith's back. They had managed to bribe some warriors with trade goods, and these braves were busily making preparations for murder.

It seems likely that Powhatan knew of the plot, although he himself had no part in it. It is probable that he knew how strong the colony was becoming and would not have been displeased if the murder of its leader caused the settlement to fail, even though that leader was his personal friend. In any case, on the day the attempt was to be made Powhatan was not around; he had withdrawn discreetly into the forest.

At first, all went as usual. Some of the party felled trees while others shaped them into boards. The carpenters were already at work on the second story of the house. Although some of the workers actually knew nothing at all about the scheme, most did. Those who did not wish to be involved had been warned by the plotters to keep out of the way or risk being killed along with Smith.

Everyone normally worked until late in the morning, when they stopped for a light meal of cold food. According to Smith, he had been supervising the work on the second story when he realized it was time to stop and eat. He and John Russell climbed down and began walking back to the campsite. Suddenly at least a dozen warriors ran at them from all sides, screaming and brandishing spears and knives.

He and Russell drew their weapons and stood back to back. Then began another of Smith's incredible battles. It would seem, from the way he describes it, that he enjoyed hand-to-hand combat almost as much as he enjoyed telling about it afterwards. Lack of practice had not dulled his skill at either.

Smith drew both pistols, took aim with one, and fired, blowing off the head of a Chickahominy warrior who was supposedly one of Powhatan's advisers. If this is true, it would indicate that the sachem was closely involved in the plot. With his second shot Smith killed another warrior. Naturally, Russell did not do quite as well as Smith. He killed his first warrior but only wounded a second.

During all of this thirty-eight colonists remained at the unfinished house, in full view. Not one came to help. Some of them wanted to but were prevented by the plotters, mostly Dutch, who drew their pistols and threatened to shoot anyone who went to Smith's aid.

Smith did not care. Although his pistols were empty he had drawn his ever-present scimitar and was having a good time hacking away at his enemies. Presumably Russell was doing the same thing with his sword. Neither would have had an opportunity during all this fuss to reload his firearms. They would have had to depend on their swords and their skill, which would seem to have been more than adequate.

One brave, who should have known better, tried to jump Smith and was immediately cut down. Then the intrepid captain took off the arm of another who had the same idea.

Russell was doing only a little less well than Smith, and was keeping the Indians at bay. But holding them off just was not enough, and Smith knew it. Suddenly he went berserk. He ran forward, away from the astonished Russell, whirling his scimitar in the air over his head. The Indians were horrified at being attacked by one man whose blade moved too rapidly to be seen as more than a blur. Before they knew what was happening, he had killed one man and wounded another. Deciding that discretion was indeed the better part of valor, the remaining warriors fled, leaving their dead behind.

Smith knew they could not take the time then to discuss the plot and the traitors. There were hundreds more warriors in the nearby Chickahominy village, and if they decided to take up the fray where their comrades had left off, there would be no hope for any of the settlers. Smith ordered them all into military formation, and then, surprisingly, had them march toward the Chickahominy town. They raided the Indians' stores, Smith says, taking all the corn and venison they could carry. This tale sounds questionable, as it seems unlikely the Indians would have left the stores completely unguarded.

Nevertheless, Smith says, his men made several trips to the two shallops, which were riding at anchor nearby. Smith, Russell, and four others stood guard. The loading continued until both boats actually sat low in the water.

Then the party collected all its tools and equipment and carried them to the shallops also. They then sailed back to Jamestown.

Powhatan's house was never completed. Smith considered himself justified both in breaking the deal and in taking as much food as he could because the sachem's warriors had attacked him. Powhatan and Smith never met again face to face.

Once they reached Jamestown Smith took prompt action. The food was carried safely into the settlement's warehouses. Then Smith ordered the plotters arrested. Only three Dutchmen and two Englishmen were taken into custody. At the trial several weeks later, one of the Englishmen was cleared of all charges. The other four plotters were convicted and sentenced to be given fifty strokes with a whip, a very severe penalty. The sentences were not carried out until much later.

More immediate was Smith's concern with possible retaliation by the Chickahominy. They had lost a lot of food, and Smith certainly expected a reaction of some sort from Powhatan. He ordered an alert sounded and the gates closed. Watches were organized at the fort, and the community prepared for a siege.

Nothing happened. Powhatan sent no warriors against Jamestown. He did not even send messengers. Possibly he regretted his part in the plot, probably he felt that Smith was within his rights to take the food, if indeed Smith did take as much as he claimed. In any case, the Chickahominy kept their distance.

The settlement had no dealings at all with the Indian confederation until springtime. Individual Chickahominy began showing up when the weather warmed, bringing furs from animals they had trapped over the winter, hoping to barter. Until that time both sides avoided each other. The colonists could not afford a fight, and neither they nor the Indians wanted to be responsible for a war. When relations resumed, no mention was made of the attempted murder. Everyone acted as if nothing out of the ordinary had taken place.

It is possible that the incident had unexpected good results. The tale of Smith's prowess probably grew in the telling, not just in Smith's own version but among the Indians as well. The tribes undoubtedly respected such strength but were also curious about it. Indians from every part of the region began appearing with corn, venison, and smoked fish, which they offered at reasonable barter rates, probably hoping to get a look at Smith in the bargain. As a result the colonists ate well all winter, and the warehouses had not been emptied by spring. For one winter, at least, Jamestown was not threatened with starvation.

 **20**

THERE were no Indian troubles in the first months of 1609, but the council had its hands full with other matters. The incident at Paspahegh had shocked them. It was outrageous that a small handful of men could hold off more than thirty loyal colonists and keep them from coming to the aid of Smith and Russell when they were attacked by the Indians. The schedule of military training was stepped up as a result. Dissatisfaction grew among the settlers.

Smith knew of their complaints but ignored them. He was not given to democratic ideals, and he felt the increased training could only benefit the colony. The situation was far more serious than he realized, however. Scrivener had been plotting against him, trying to persuade other members of the council to join him in a plan to depose Smith. When Percy came to Smith secretly with this tale, the president found it hard to believe. After all, he had placed full trust in Scrivener, and had chosen the man for his personal deputy. But when John Russell, now a loyal friend, told him the same thing, and it was confirmed by Peter Winne, the new council member, he had to believe it. He was also informed that

Richard Waldo, the other new member, was in on the plot as well.

Smith knew he had to bring the matter up with Scrivener, but he was reluctant to do so. He decided to wait until Scrivener returned from a fishing trip he had planned. Scrivener was taking Waldo, two other gentlemen, and five commoners with him in the gig from the *Discovery*. Smith never saw them alive again.

About thirty-six hours after the little party sailed, a fierce gale hit the coast. The men failed to return, and fears for their safety mounted. Then, after about five days of waiting, a small party of Indians arrived at Jamestown with news. The gig had been found driven ashore on the east bank of Chesapeake Bay. Two bodies were later recovered, but the rest were all lost at sea.

It was really Smith's duty to examine and list the personal belongings of the victims and decide what should be done with them, but he insisted that Percy and Winne go along with him. He was glad they were with him when he found Scrivener's diary. Scrivener had written at length of his plan to depose Smith and have himself elected president. Smith was shocked, and for the rest of his life was skeptical of the value of friendship.

There was far less work to be done during the winter months. Working hours were cut back, giving extra hours of leisure. The additional free time did not turn out to be a benefit. With less to do the men became bored, and many spent time brooding, waiting for spring. Pigs and chickens had been part of Newport's last cargo, and they were put in the charge of one group of colonists. These men planned to take two of the animals out into the forest, kill them, and roast them away from the others. Smith found out about the scheme before the men could carry it out, and he realized that immediate action was needed to preserve discipline in the bored little community.

Smith called a meeting of everyone in the community, not just the council, and made a speech. He said that it was foolish for them to believe that the investors in London could completely support the colony indefinitely, nor could they continue to rely solely on Smith's efforts. In the past the labor of forty workers had supported 150 idle colonists. In the future all must be industrious. To ensure this result, Smith laid down a new law: "He that will not worke shall not eate," he relates in *A Map of Virginia.*

Furthermore, said Smith, anyone who doubted that he had full authority over them had only to read the "Letters patent" on which the colony was founded to realize the contrary. Smith ordered the letters read publicly each week, just in case anyone forgot. Anyone who broke the law could expect prompt punishment.

This was the right time, Smith thought, for the whipping of the three Dutchmen and the Englishman who had incited the Chickahominy against him. The sentence was carried out on the day following his speech, in the presence of all the male members of the colony. The women were not forced to attend.

A platform had been erected at one end of Smith Field for the purpose, and thirty armed men guarded it. The executioner wore a black hood over his head, in the style of London's royal hangmen, so that no one knew who he was. It was a thoroughly unpleasant spectacle, with no one but the prisoners making a sound. If one of them lost consciousness, he was brought around again by a bucket

132

of cold water. When it was over the prisoners were removed to the fort, where they were treated by a doctor. The men then dispersed for lunch, but no one was hungry. Smith had made his point.

To further help the men remember their duties, he posted a schedule in the common room of the fort. This chart listed the name of every man, his duties for the week, and those duties he had fulfilled. Each group was supervised by a council member, who made the necessary remarks and notations on the chart. There was no problem; everyone had become very industrious.

Smith set the men to making improvements in the community during the winter months. The drinking water had had a brackish taste, due to the settlement's location in marshy land, and the men had complained. Wells were dug, and the quality of the water improved.

Twenty-two new houses were built. The church was reroofed, an operation it badly needed. During bad weather outdoor work could not be done, so the men made fish nets from vines, following the example of the nearby coastal tribes.

The town's defenses were also improved. Smith had them build a blockhouse on the narrow point of land that connected the peninsula with the mainland. Two small cannon were placed there, and men were given sentry duty around the clock. It was now possible for men to work in the fields beyond the palisades of the town without posting guards all around for fear of a surprise attack.

There was still concern over the possibility of a Spanish attack, so another blockhouse was built downriver, on what became known as Hogs' Island. The men watching there had a good view of the sea and could give warning in plenty of time if the Spanish were planning to launch an assault. Smith wanted to be prepared for any contingency.

The food situation continued to improve, in part thanks to Newport's last cargo. Three sows had been brought to the colony, and the pig population was growing rapidly. Twenty-five chickens and roosters had also been on board; now the colony had more than six hundred chickens, and they were continuing to multiply. Eggs, once rare, were commonplace.

There was one serious problem, in the form of rats. The rodents were stealing corn from the warehouses and were an ever-present source of possible disease. Their numbers also continued to multiply, and no method of control or extermination that the colonists tried had any success. A few cats would have solved the problem, but there were none in the town. Smith made a note to ask the next ship's captain to leave them a few cats (every ship had a few).

The success of the colony was still largely dependent on the goodwill of the Indians, and Smith knew it. By the spring of 1609 he felt the colony was secure and well enough organized for him to concentrate on their relations with the natives. He invited the sachems and under-sachems of different tribes to visit Jamestown and attend feasts given in their honor. They were pleased to accept, and Smith treated them with elaborate courtesy. He gave them gifts and served them the best food from Jamestown's supplies. The settlers were busy with their many guests.

Powhatan did not come to any of the festivities. He did send one of his sons in his place, and Smith treated him gravely, with perfect courtesy. He could not resist, however, sending Powhatan a gift: two hammers, a saw, and a keg of nails. The implication was that Powhatan might want to put his own people to work finishing the house. After all, it was the Chickahominy who were responsible for the disruption of its construction. No one knows if the house was ever completed.

Smith's policy of generosity to the Indians paid off well. Trade relations were cemented with all the nations in the region, and the Indians were glad to bring corn, venison, and other supplies to the settlement because they knew they would receive a good price. The trade in furs also increased significantly. Jamestown was finally becoming self-sufficient.

One unpleasant incident occurred that spring, initiated by one of the Dutch settlers. His name is spelled variously as Francis, Fraunce, or France. He was an ambitious man with little regard for the possible long-range consequences of his actions. He knew the Indians were fascinated with the firearms of the newcomers and were anxious to obtain them. He believed he could make a small fortune by dealing them arms, if he could keep his fellow colonists from finding out. He therefore began to steal muskets, gunpowder, and ammunition from the fort's arsenal. He took his supplies out into the forest and buried them, hoping to keep his actions secret until he had acquired enough to make a large trade, one that would bring him a fortune in furs for the European market. He could not have expected to be able to make any further trades.

Francis was not very subtle. He stole significant quantities of the materials he needed. John Russell, who was in charge of keeping the arsenal's inventory, discovered first the loss of a large amount of powder. He reported this to Smith, who wasted no time. He called every member of the community into the president's office, one by one, for questioning.

Francis could not hold up under questioning. When interrogated, he broke down and admitted his thefts. He told Smith his hiding places, and the stolen ammunition was recovered. Francis was sentenced severely, but not as harshly as he might have been. He was given a public whipping and a jail term and was ordered to be deported on the next ship that stopped at Jamestown.

The health of the settlers also improved dramatically during this period. Two settlers, one a man named Leigh and the other Peter Winne, developed fevers and died, but most of the town remained healthy. The well water was purer, and they were now adequately fed and housed. The men had also become accustomed to the conditions of life in the New World and had developed resistance to disease. Smith sincerely hoped there would be no more epidemics and wrote this in a report to the directors.

The weather was pleasant in the spring of 1609, and nature was kind to the colony. There was such a variety and abundance of berries that it was possible to make jams, which were put away in the warehouses. The forest was teeming with deer and bear, which were shot, and some of the more adventurous hunters of the colony went inland after buffalo. Large flocks of wildfowl paused in their northward journeys to rest on the nearby lakes and ponds, and groups of colonists were kept busy snaring them by the hundreds. Schools of sturgeon and shad swam up the James River and were caught. The shad were eaten fresh; the sturgeon were smoked and sometimes mixed into pemmican. The colony was now a safe and pleasant place to live.

 **21**

A friendly ship sailed up the James River on July 10, 1609, reported to the settlement by the cannon in the blockhouse on Hogs' Island, which were fired three times. Smith, like the other colonists, prepared to receive the news from home. Smith had no way of knowing that there was a very unpleasant surprise in store for him.

The ship was under the command of Captain Samuel Argal, a burly, red-bearded man with hypnotic black eyes. Argal is sometimes described as a villain, but he was not. He was not in any way tactful and was impetuous and bluntly narrow-minded, so candid that he was brutal, but he was not a bully.

Argal had brought with him provisions, tools, bolts of cloth, and many other things the settlers at Jamestown badly needed. He also brought a letter to Captain John Smith from the directors of the Company. He told Smith to prepare himself for a shock and then moved back to watch Smith's reaction.

The letters indicated a great change for the future of the Virginia colony. They began by criticizing Smith for his mistreatment of the Indian tribes. Smith knew the charges were unsubstantiated and that the directors must have been fed false information. He subsequently learned that Gabriel Archer and John Ratcliffe, his old enemies, were responsible for the allegations.

The directors also expressed thorough dissatisfaction with the cargoes Smith had been sending back to England. They said they expected higher quality. Although they accepted the furs and the sassafras, which brought excellent prices in England, they called the tar and glass shipments inadequate, said they wanted more lumber, and hinted that they considered Smith guilty of mismanagement. They indicated that they thought he might somehow be making a profit at their expense, although they could not say how. They showed no understanding of the colony's problems, despite all Smith had written them concerning the real situation of the settlement.

It was the final portions of the letter that held the really crushing news. King James himself had at last become personally interested in the project. He had directed his Privy Council to use Crown funds to ensure the growth, well-being, and security of the colony. The incredible number of nine ships was soon to set sail for the New World, to carry between five and six hundred new settlers to Virginia. The settlers would be both men and women, and they would soon be followed by others as well, with all of their expenses paid by the Crown.

It was obvious that a vastly expanded colony of this type would need a new sort of government, a new administration. The directors of the London Company were sending one of their own number to Virginia to become the Royal Governor. He was Thomas West, Baron De La Warr, a competent administrator and a good soldier. Smith would not have minded working under him, even though his presence and that of his wife would have meant a miniature viceregal court would be established in the colony.

A large governmental staff was accompanying De La Warr to the New World, and each of its many members had been given an imposing title. Sir George Somers, a knight, was a Rear Admiral in the Royal Navy. He had been as quick to promote his interests at court as he was competent at sea. As a result, he had been named Admiral of the New World Fleet. Sir Thomas Gates, a baronet, would be appointed Lieutenant Governor. Sir Thomas Dale, another baronet, whose family was highly influential at court, would be the High Marshal, a post combining the duties of both military commander-in-chief and chief of police. Sir Thomas was a likeable man who had had very limited military experience. Many were amused by his appointment, but he later proved himself a hard-working and valuable deputy to Lord De La Warr. Sir Ferdinando Wainman, a knight, was given the title of General of Horse, which was rather grandiose as there was no mention in the letter of sending any horses as mounts for cavalry. Captain Newport was to return to Jamestown permanently as Vice Admiral of the fleet.

Smith, who had done so much for Jamestown, would be removed from office and would have no further responsibilities. The council was to be disbanded also. If any of them wished to remain in Virginia, they would have to do so as private citizens. Smith would remain in office as technical president until De La Warr arrived, at which time he would retire into private life. The directors showed no gratitude for what Smith had done, and they made enemies of his council by making no attempt to soothe feelings that would obviously be hurt by the news. They did not express any thanks at all for what the men had done.

In a postscript was the bitterest message of all. Gabriel Archer and John Ratcliffe, the veteran troublemakers, were returning to the New World to live. So was John Martin, who had recovered from his illness. Martin claimed to know something no one else did, namely, the location of secret hidden gold mines. The directors apparently believed him. The directors did not know it, but they were sending back a load of trouble for the new governors of the Virginia colony.

Someone else might have given up and sailed home on Argal's ship, but Smith would not. He had the investment of all his years of hard labor to protect, and he would not leave his duty. He was still president until De La Warr came to relieve him, and he intended to stay until then.

Percy and other gentlemen-adventurers were not at all happy with the decrees from London and were threatening to rebel. In response to this Smith, who could easily have filled Argal's hold with furs and lumber for the return voyage, ordered the port closed. He assured the disgruntled colonists that this way they would have a sure passage back to England if the situation became unbearable. Argal had to remain in Jamestown for the present, and all shipping was to be frozen.

The colony, which had just begun to do so well, now had its luck change for the worse. The ships of the squadron sailing for the New World were struck by a hurricane in the area of Bermuda, and several were forced to land there. All of the ships suffered heavy damage. Passengers were lost overboard in the storm and supplies were damaged; many immigrants lost their lives to an

141

unknown illness. Even the majority of the crews on the vessels became ill. It was a wonder that any of them managed to make port at all.

In the early morning hours of August 3, 1609, a battered ship was seen making its way up the James River. The crew of the unhappy vessel, ironically named the *Blessing*, had never expected to reach Virginia. Within eight days the *Blessing* was followed by the *Lion*, the *Falcon*, and the *Unity*. The *Unity* was in the worst condition of all. Many of her passengers were dead. Of the seventy who remained alive, all were ill. All the crew were ill, too, with the exception only of the master and two sailors, who brought the ship in.

A few days after this the *Diamond* arrived. Two of the passengers on the *Diamond* were Archer and Ratcliffe. Both were anxious for vengeance against Smith, whom they considered responsible for their past disgrace.

The facilities of Jamestown were severely strained by the arrival of several hundred sick, hungry, and helpless men and women. They were all too sick to work, and it looked as though the supplies in the warehouses, which had been built up with so much hard work, would be depleted in a few short weeks.

Both Archer and Ratcliffe could not wait to make a bad situation even worse. Neither was affected by illness, and they took advantage of their health to begin immediately trying to undermine Smith's authority. No sooner had they landed than they began spreading the word that Smith was no longer president. They demanded that Lord De La Warr's younger brother, a gentleman named West, be given the position of temporary acting governor.

There would have been no trouble if De La Warr's

ship had been among the arrivals, but neither the governor nor any of the other newly appointed officials had reached the colony yet. Their ship the *Sea Venture*, flagship of the new fleet, had been blown far off course by the hurricane. It was to be months before any of the new high officials would reach the shores of Virginia.

It was therefore still up to Smith to do his best to cope with all problems. As soon as the new immigrants were well enough to do any work, they were set to building more houses. The directors had paid as little attention to Smith's advice regarding the type of settlers suited to the New World as they had to his other suggestions. Most of the new colonists were of the same sort as the old: eager fortune hunters anxious to get rich as rapidly as possible, then go home. They were unused to discipline and had no desire whatever to work at farming, lumbering, or fishing.

Smith had to take prompt action to keep the situation in hand. To begin with, he placed Archer and Ratcliffe under house arrest. He was supported in this action by all the community's veteran settlers, both gentlemen and commoners, who were not slow to remember previous troubles. Although he could have granted them parole, under his authority as president, the last thing Smith wanted was to have them wandering around Jamestown stirring up trouble. He placed troops at the door of their house to be sure they did not mingle with the other settlers.

He then assigned houses to married couples and put one end of a compound at the disposal of the unmarried women. He posted guards for them and instructed them not to go out alone until conditions became more settled.

Smith then decided to try to kill two birds with one

stone. It was obvious that the colony would need a lot more food very soon, and it was also obvious that the rowdy newcomers needed a little discipline and work. Smith decided that the best solution to both problems was to send 120 of the new colonists to the falls of the James River, with a few of the veteran settlers as guides. Once there, they were to clear land and start a new plantation. Each of the men would be assigned his own field to cultivate, but in the beginning all would live together in a blockhouse they would construct. The initial clearing of the land would not be too difficult; Smith had selected an area of fertile meadowlands with only a few trees.

There were still plenty of would-be gold-seekers left in Jamestown, so Smith sent them off to the lands near the Nansemond. Their project was the same as that of the earlier group: to clear forest and start still another plantation.

If Smith were discouraged or disappointed by the recent turn of events, he did not admit it to anyone, nor did he put his thoughts on paper. He certainly had far too much to do to spend time brooding. He sent Percy and Russell inland to barter for food with the Indians, not only for corn and venison but for any vegetables and meat available. He was concerned that Jamestown's expansion might bring about hostilities with Powhatan's confederation, but he felt there was no longer any choice. Jamestown now had nearly eight hundred inhabitants and they needed more crops and more territory.

Unfortunately, this plan almost brought about a major war immediately. Smith found out, from a series of discouraging reports, that the men who had gone to the land near the river falls had broken native rules of conduct. They had spent a night near a Chickahominy village and had not hesitated to take anything they needed, without informing the Indians. Apparently they had stolen weapons, clothing, food, and cooking utensils. The Chickahominy were naturally upset, and Smith realized he would probably have to make a personal trip as a diplomatic gesture to restore normal friendly relations.

The necessity for the trip was urgent, but so were many other affairs. It was impossible for Smith to handle everything at once, and he knew he had to leave behind someone responsible to take charge of the affairs of the colony. He called a meeting of the council and suggested that a successor be chosen to hold office in his place until De La Warr arrived. He expected the new Governor any day, and his own term of office was drawing to a close. He suggested John Martin for the post, and the council unanimously approved his choice. Martin was also to take charge during Smith's absence on his journey to the interior. Before Smith left, he made sure everyone was hard at work hunting, fishing, gathering wild berries, or building houses.

Smith took one of the shallops up the James River, stopping at every Chickahominy village along the way to distribute gifts and talk with the people. He asked for nothing in return, and his gesture mollified the Indians, as had been intended.

When he reached the site the colonists had chosen he had a lot of work to do. The plantation was on poor ground, so he had it moved to a higher level. Smith supervised while they built houses, a fort, and a palisade, and he had them begin clearing another two hundred acres for planting crops. While the men were engaged in these activities Smith visited the nearby Indians, working out barter arrangements so that the settlers would have an additional, if small, source of food. This would be especially necessary during the winter months if some of their own crops failed.

September was drawing to a close before Smith took the shallop and went back downriver toward Jamestown. He had only a few companions with him.

Most of the colonists had adopted the Indians' habit of smoking tobacco in a pipe. One night while Smith slept, one of the settlers accidentally set fire to Smith's gunpowder bag while lighting his own pipe with a tinderbox and flint. The resulting explosion sheathed Smith in flames.

Smith awoke immediately, and owed his life to his subsequent quick thinking. He jumped at once into the river below the shallop, but discovered that he had been burned so severly that he was unable to swim. Some of the men threw him a line and pulled him back to the boat. When they were eventually able to get him out of the water, they discovered that he had very serious burns on his legs, stomach, and chest.

Not much could be done for Smith before they reached Jamestown, and he was in horrible pain. Once back in the settlement he was treated by a doctor with soothing salves, but this remedy was not very effective. For several days his life was in doubt.

Smith insisted, however, on being informed of the colony's affairs even though he was incapacitated and in bed. The doctors told him that he needed rest, but he ignored their advice as much as he could. When Martin and members of the council came to see him, he insisted on talking over the business of the colony and demanded that they come to confer with him several times a day. He was still in excruciating pain, but he was conscious, so he worked. He was unwilling to trust all the details of administration to others while he was still technically in charge.

Almost all of Jamestown was hoping for Smith's recovery. There were two outstanding exceptions, however: Ratcliffe and Archer. They were to face a new trial on conspiracy charges, and they were very concerned. If Smith lived, which looked likely, they knew they could not escape conviction, and if they were convicted they were likely to be deported. Deportation to England for a second time would completely ruin their careers.

When it seemed certain that Smith would indeed survive, the two conspirators resorted to desperate measures. They hired two men named Coe and Dyer to creep into Smith's house at night and shoot him in his bed. Fortunately, this plan was not carried out. Ratcliffe and Archer would not take the direct risks themselves, and Coe and Dyer, when faced with the actual prospect of killing, lost their courage. They gave themselves up, and were arrested. The next day they confessed fully to Martin, who ordered that they, too, be brought to trial.

In the meantime it had become obvious that Smith needed more medical treatment than he could receive in Virginia. Martin, Percy, and other friends persuaded him to return to England. The *Sea Venture* was still expected daily, bringing the new colonial officials, including the Governor. Smith was in such great pain that there was little he could do for the colony until they arrived, in any case. He agreed to the proposal.

Smith was exhausted. His injuries had weakened him, and he was tired by the effort required to keep turning aside the attempts of his enemies to harm him. The Company's directors had failed to realize all he had done for them and for the Jamestown colony, and they showed no signs of changing those policies that he knew were not good. He wanted to go back to England and rest, at least for a while.

Three of the ships had been refitted and were ready to sail again, loaded with timber, furs, and herbs, which Smith had ordered brought on board. On the fourth of October Smith was carried on board the *Unity*. Most of the colonists were there to see him off, many of them weeping. But a few were not sorry to see him go, and even as the ships sailed down the river they prepared a list of false charges against him, to be sent back later to the Company's directors in England.

Smith was so sick that he slept while the *Unity* made its way down the James River and out into the Atlantic. He did not know it, but he had missed his last chance to look back at the shores of his beloved Virginia. He was not to see the Virginia again.

 **22**

AFTER Smith left the colony, the welfare of Jamestown took an abrupt turn for the worse, such had been the importance of his presence and his contributions to the stability of the settlement. There was a notable absence of real leadership. Martin tried to establish order and failed. He was followed by Percy, who did not succeed either. Percy, whose account was later published by Smith in his *Generall Historie of Virginia,* wrote that no one was willing to accept any authority, and so many men connived against him that there "are now twenty Presidents."

The food situation was even worse. The colonists would not accept rationing, lacking the foresight to plan for the approaching winter. Food was even stolen from the warehouses, and the thieves were never caught. Relations with Powhatan's confederation deteriorated, which may have sown seeds for a massacre of colonists that took place several years later. In any case, there was no one left to trade with the Indians for food. Smith had been the only accomplished diplomat in the community.

The inevitable result of these chaotic conditions became known as the "starving time" in Virginia. The winter of 1609–10, which had looked so promising before

Smith left, proved to be a complete disaster. When Smith sailed for England there had been 573 settlers; by mid-May 1610 there were only 61 remaining.

The gentlemen stole pigs and chickens for their private use when they could, and left the commoners to fend for themselves. Hungry settlers combed the beaches for oysters, clams, and mussels. If they ventured into the forest the Indians, whose relations with the colony had soured, killed them. Even the late crop of nuts and berries thus became unavailable to them.

Most horrible of all, as Percy relates in Smith's *Generall Historie*, is the state to which the last survivors were reduced. Although they tried for a while to exist "for the most part, by roots, herbes, acornes, walnuts, berries, now and then a little fish," they finally ended by eating "one another boyled and stewed with roots and herbs." Although this account was published a decade and a half after the "starving time," it greatly shocked its readers. Only Lord De La Warr's arrival in June 1610, with new settlers and supplies, saved the colony from extinction.

It was during this dreadful winter that the name of Pocahontas surfaces in the works of authors other than John Smith. Most notable is the account Percy gives of a teenage boy named Henry Spelman who wandered into the wilderness. The son of the noted English scholar Henry Spelman, the youth became so hungry that he ignored caution and went far inland in search of food. Spelman, who survived the winter, returned to England in 1614. He wrote of his adventure in a little pamphlet titled *An Account of the Starving Time in Virginia*, which was published in London late in the year. It attracted very little attention, but it was probably read by John Smith.

150

Spelman describes how, wandering in search of food, he became lost and was eventually found and taken into custody by the Chickahominy. The Indian nation was no longer feeling particularly kindly toward the interlopers, and they would have killed the youth. Pocahontas exercised her right of position, however, and spared the boy's life, thus adopting him. Spelman was thereafter treated with the utmost kindness by everyone, including Powhatan himself. He eventually returned to Jamestown well fed, and thus considerably luckier than his fellow colonists.

The great similarity of Spelman's story and Smith's later account of his meeting and relationship with Pocahontas is marked enough to be suspicious. Although it is impossible to prove, it is possible that Smith appropriated Spelman's tale and enlarged on it. It would have been hard for a man of Smith's imaginative talent to ignore such an idea, especially considering the impact Pocahontas was having on London society at the time.

When Lord De La Warr finally reached Jamestown in late May 1610, with Sir Thomas Gates and Sir George Somers, he was just in time. He brought with him 150 new colonists and enough provisions to rescue the emaciated survivors of the "starving time." These unfortunates had been about to abandon Jamestown entirely. After enduring a living nightmare for seven months they had decided to try to reach England in the delapidated ship *Discovery.*

After that, ships arrived on regular schedules from England, and the settlement no longer had to face such a great danger. De La Warr was a good and competent administrator who quickly put the colony back on its feet. Order was restored, and a new era of rapid growth

151

was inaugurated. Both the Crown and the directors of the London Company poured funds into the enterprise at last, and Virginia slowly regained its strength. It still took many years of hard work, however, before the colony became as comfortable and secure as it had been when John Smith had been its president.

Smith himself was in no condition to worry much about Jamestown, or anything else, on his long voyage back to London. The trip lasted eight weeks, during which the ship *Unity* was tossed by autumn gales. It was impossible for the injured Smith to remain still and rest in bed, and his burns tortured him unremittingly. For a period of about ten days he became delirious. When he was lucid again he was still so ill that he could not take any nourishment other than "a few biscuits and a little barley water."

When the *Unity* finally made its way up the Thames to anchor at the London wharves in time for the Christmas season of 1609, Smith was a changed man. Although he was healing, he was still suffering from his burns, and he was so heavily bandaged that he was able to walk only with great difficulty. He came ashore in shabby armor and patched clothes and worn boots, completely unlike the heroic figure he had last presented in England. Although he was not yet thirty years old, his hair was turning gray and he walked uncertainly, like a sick old man.

All of Smith's belongings from the New World were packed in two sea chests. In one were his clothing and weapons, all so old as to be almost valueless. In the other were Smith's most precious possessions: his manuscripts, charts, maps, and detailed notes, and all the papers he had gathered since the beginning of his voyage to the New World three years before. These items were priceless, and he knew it.

Smith was totally ignored by the directors of the London Company, although at first he considered the possibility that they would take seriously the claims of his enemies and bring criminal charges against him. They did not, and no one in England recognized the value of his contributions to the colony of Jamestown. He had worked hard to create a community in a far distant wilderness, but no one was on hand to greet him when he left the ship.

Smith, too ill to walk, hired a chair to carry him, plus two men to take his chests through London. Ill and weak, he set off in search of lodging in a cold London rain. Although London probably seemed unchanged to him, he was no doubt thinking of Virginia again. He had become addicted to the New World, which would continue to enthrall him as long as he lived.

 **23**

SMITH recovered his health very slowly and painfully. Depressed and ill, he took inexpensive rooms in a small house on a little lane near the Thames. For three months he saw no one but the doctor, whose daily services were necessary. He hired a boy for the sole purpose of bringing him his meals from nearby taverns, thus avoiding going out into the streets. He was unable to enjoy the English beef or the English beer for which he had longed during his years in Virginia, for the physician deemed it unwise for him to eat heavy foods. His burns healed very slowly, leaving permanent scars, but he gradually regained his health, and with it his vitality.

Nothing could lift his depression, however. He brooded constantly about Jamestown, which he regarded as an expensive experiment. He wrote, in the *Generall Historie*, that he had spent nearly five years of hard work, plus "more than five hundred pounds of my own estate, for which there is no recompense; beside all the dangers, miseries, and encumbrances and loss of other employment I endured gratis." He was happy in the knowledge that he had left the more than five hundred men and women who had been under his charge well provided for. Not until later did he learn of the disaster that struck after his departure; if he had known of it during the period of his recovery his spirits would undoubtedly have been even more depressed.

Smith made no attempt to contact the directors of the London Company. They had displayed grave lack of confidence in him, as well as total misunderstanding of the problems involved in settling the New World. He was so disturbed and dispirited that he did not try to explain the true situation in person, nor even contact them to clear his own name.

He wrote briefly to his sister and brother, telling them that he had returned to England, but he made no arrangements to see them. He contacted no friends, and he did not even try to reach the publisher of *A True Relation*. The book had created a sensation, as he had learned from Captain Argal, but for a while he showed no interest in it. Eventually, though, he had to; the book was earning him large sums of money.

In the meantime, however, he was finding it difficult, as his health improved, to live like a hermit in the middle of England's busy capital. For a man of flamboyant nature he had been remarkably subdued for years. Inevitably he got in touch again with Frances, Duchess of Richmond, and they resumed their affair.

Frances was shocked by the state in which Smith was living, by his drab apartment and his mental depression, and she began a campaign to force him to become more active. To begin with, she enlisted the help of her husband, who undoubtedly knew of the affair, in finding better lodgings for Smith. Smith did not have furniture sufficient for the large suite of rooms she found, so Frances loaned him some of her own furnishings.

155

Frances also forced him to take an interest in the success of *A True Relation*. He was delighted when she informed him that it was the most popular book in England at the time, and he needed no further urging to visit his printer, George Hall on Fleet Street. Hall gave him the astonishing news that his book had already earned over one thousand pounds, a significant sum, and was continuing to sell rapidly. The directors of the London Company might have treated him unjustly and continue to ignore him, but the people of England loved his book. Smith's self-esteem received a much-needed boost. The popularity of *A True Relation* had the added benefit of giving extensive publicity to the Jamestown colony and encouraging more immigrants to apply to the London Company to go to the New World.

It is possible that Smith expected an apology for his shabby treatment from the directors of the London Company, or at least some form of recognition from them, before he would consent to meet with them. He never bothered to explain himself in this regard; apparently he took it for granted that readers of his later books would understand his feelings completely without explanation, or that no explanation was appropriate. Frances took the initiative in this matter also, and arranged a private dinner party at the Richmond town palace. She invited only Smith and Richard Hakluyt, and at the end of the meal she and her husband withdrew, leaving the two alone.

Hakluyt had not been in total agreement with the stand taken by some of his fellow directors, wealthy and powerful nobles with a different outlook from his own. He listened with great interest to Smith's account of the true state of affairs in the Jamestown colony. Although nothing definite is known of the conversation that night, it is reasonable to assume that Hakluyt gave Smith's recital a sympathetic reception. He had always been skeptical of the possibilities for finding an easily accessible store of gold or other wealth in America, and his chief interest was in the discovery of a sea passage to the Pacific.

Hakluyt was willing to accept Smith's opinion that there was no river that crossed the continent either in Virginia itself or in the regions immediately to the north. He agreed to meet with Smith again the next day, and Smith, delighted with the Archdeacon's continued friendliness, was pleased. He arrived at the appointed time carrying his maps and charts of Virginia, the Chesapeake Bay area, and the land of the Susquehannocks, all of which he had of course drawn himself. By the time the session was over, all coolness between the two men had evaporated in a common enthusiasm for their subject.

Although Hakluyt was a scientist with a minimal interest in human relations, he was upset by what Smith had to tell him of the intrigues in Jamestown. The troublemaking of Archer and Ratcliffe particularly distressed him, and he felt that Prince Henry should be informed of what the true state of affairs in Virginia had been. Smith was reluctant to meet with Henry, feeling insulted because the Prince had ignored him. But he could not refuse a direct summons to Henry's apartments in Fleet Street for an interview, so he went, accompanied by Hakluyt.

He found the Prince of Wales attended by two of the new directors of the London Company, the Earl of Southampton and Sir Ferdinando Gorges, who had Anglicized the spelling of his surname to George. Both men were enthusiastic about the exploration and discovery of new lands. They were also of the opinion that the policy of the Dutch was wiser, in the long run, than that of the Spanish. The Dutch were becoming increasingly wealthy by trading with newly discovered peoples, whereas the gold-seeking Spaniards, who stripped territories of their available mineral resources, sometimes went bankrupt.

Smith used the opportunity to vindicate himself. It was the right time and these were the right people. Prince Henry was the most powerful man in the land, after his father King James, and the Earl of Southampton was very wealthy. Sir Ferdinando was not only rich but was also one of the few men in the realm who was a close friend of the King. Among them, if they chose, and if Smith properly impressed them, they could finance any future expeditions he might wish to undertake, and Smith was already thinking in such terms.

Smith spoke to them at length, using his notes frequently to substantiate points he felt might be in doubt. He did not allow his flair for the dramatic to run away with him, but remained persuasive and charming.

Prince Henry did not offer Smith an apology; that would have been beneath the dignity of the Prince of Wales, at least in front of other gentlemen, but he did the best he could. His own relations with his father had improved considerably, and it was within his power to arrange an audience with the King. This he did.

Within a few days Smith was summoned to Whitehall. Both the Earl of Southampton and Sir Ferdinando accompanied him, as he had made a very good impression on both of these gentlemen. They incidentally notified their fellow directors of the London Company, by this

158

action, that they both accepted and supported Smith and his position.

Smith could not have greatly enjoyed his audience. The interest of King James in the New World was limited, and he had supplied the London Company with funds only because the Prince of Wales would not leave him alone until he had donated generously from the Treasury. He appeared to be completely bored with Smith and all he had to say.

The atmosphere of the throne room was cold enough to put a damper on Smith's fiery histrionics. James was a frugal man who remembered a poverty-stricken childhood, and to him the burning of enough wood to keep the room warm was an outrageous expense. Ladies who followed the current fashions of low-cut gowns went to great lengths to avoid appearing at court, and men were permitted to wear hats as well as wigs for added warmth. King James himself seemed to suffer from a chronic, if not continuous, head cold, and kept his face hidden behind a handkerchief.

Only the King and a few favored nobles were permitted to sit, so the interview had that added discomfort. Queen Anne had a throne next to the King's but was rarely present to occupy it. The Princes Henry and Charles also had small thrones in the hall, but they found innumerable excuses to absent themselves. If James was especially pleased with someone, he would be asked to sit for the interview. John Smith stood the whole time.

After first receiving the summons to the audience, Smith planned a strong plea for a plan of sensible colonization of the New World. But Frances convinced him that the King would not appreciate such a speech, and Prince Henry gave him the same advice independently.

Most people found it difficult to speak with James in any case. He was a lackluster man who had the misfortune to follow the brilliant and enormously popular Elizabeth to the throne, and he was conscious of the unfavorable comparison.

James looked down his long runny nose at Smith, asked brief, disinterested questions, and seemed to pay no attention to the answers. He yawned, scratched, and sent pages off for the hard candy he enjoyed.

Smith carefully answered each question, not letting his flair for drama rise to the surface at all. He did not speak softly, however, having been warned by Henry that the room had an acoustical problem, and the thick hanging tapestries would muffle much of what was said. Ordinarily it was difficult for anyone standing ten feet away from the King to hear much of what was going on. Smith knew that some of the directors of the London Company were in the hall, and he wanted to be sure they heard clearly every word. He spoke in tones ordinarily reserved for the drill field. Everyone heard him.

The audience lasted only thirty or forty minutes. King James signaled its end by doffing his hat, and Smith bowed and backed from the room. He was certain the whole interview had been a dismal failure.

In an anteroom he was joined by Sir Ferdinando and Southampton. Together they went to the apartments in the palace that Prince Henry was using once again, where a buffet meal, complete with rare wines, was about to be served. Many directors of the London Company were present, among them Sir John Popham, instigator of the great gold searches. Smith was now able to express himself with a good deal less restraint than he had been forced to use with the King. The idea for the party was probably Prince Henry's, who took it upon himself to create this opportunity for Smith. Smith now had the chance to speak privately with those men who had been so critical of his performance in Jamestown, and to attempt to set matters right. At Whitehall no notes were taken and no records of conversations were kept.

It is not known which of the directors were at the party, for to reveal the guest list would have been an insult to royal hospitality. A significant number were present, however, and at the end of the evening Smith went with Prince Henry and Sir Ferdinando to the lodging of Archdeacon Hakluyt. Hakluyt never bothered to attend royal parties and hardly ever appeared at audiences with the King.

Smith had now been able to explain the facts of the Jamestown colony to a number of the stockholders of the London Company. When the directors called a formal meeting in May 1610 they invited Smith, but the get-together was anticlimactic. The feud was already over, and the investors had already reached a sensible conclusion. Smith appeared in the capacity of an adviser and was treated with the greatest courtesy. Not one word of censure against him appeared in the minutes of the meeting.

The London Company planned to expand its Virginia colony, sending even more settlers and supplies to Jamestown. Smith told them at length of the richness of the Virginia resources of timber and furs, advising them to concentrate their efforts in these areas. He stressed again that he knew of no gold or silver or gems in the region, and added that the Indians wore no jewelry made of these materials.

161

Once again Smith made his case for sending artisans and farmers to the colony, stressing that adventure-seekers and those in search of easy wealth, like Archer and Ratcliffe, could destroy all the hard work he and others had put into Virginia. At about the same time Smith spoke, in that same May 1610, Lord De La Warr was finally landing at Jamestown and discovering for himself, to his horror, just how much damage undisciplined adventurers could do.

Although Smith was not rebuked, the directors did not withdraw their complaints against him, letting them stand on the record. Most of the directors obviously still had no idea of the enormous contributions Smith had made to Jamestown's survival, and he was given no praise or thanks for all of his efforts, without which the directors would have lost their New World investment. Long years would pass before the majority of the English people realized just how much Smith had done for the cause of British colonization in the New World.

Smith's position in the London Company was basically that of the outsider. Although he probably could have returned to Virginia either as a private citizen or as a minor official, Smith's dignity did not permit him to accept any position other than that of Governor, and Lord De La Warr already filled that post and was doing an excellent job. Smith's comparatively modest investment in the London Company did not entitle him to a position on the board of directors, whose current members had given vast amounts of money. If the Company eventually earned a profit, which did not appear likely for many years to come, he would earn dividends. In the meantime, however, he was treated by the nobles as a well-informed and useful former employee.

Over the course of the next few years Smith attended, from time to time, numerous meetings of the Company. The directors almost always asked for his advice and listened politely, but they did not always accept it. They took his loyalty to Jamestown for granted, with good reason, and they relied on his willingness to work hard. Unfortunately, his views of what should be done in the colony were realistic, and therefore were often at variance with those of the nobly born directors, who still knew nothing of conditions in the New World.

Smith was always honest with the directors, despite being taken for granted. He was frequently blunt to the point where he feared giving offense. One such occasion occurred when he was required to write down some of his opinions in a report. He felt obliged to attach a personal note to the completed report: "If I speak too plain, I humbly crave your pardon. But you requested me, therefore I do but my duty."

Smith was greatly frustrated by being denied the recognition he so definitely deserved. He was a man who loved praise and the limelight, and he was not satisfied that the Prince of Wales and several other highly influential men knew of his accomplishments in Virginia and appreciated them. He was justified in believing that he had done more in the cause of colonization than any other Englishman of his time, and he yearned for a reputation as great as Sir Walter Raleigh's or Sir Francis Drake's.

Probably he nursed private hopes that he would be knighted for his work in Jamestown. He had enough tact, however, not to confide his dream to Prince Henry, who would have resented it and believed he was being used. Frances, the Duchess of Richmond, knew of his

163

secret desire, however, for she hinted at it in a letter to her friend Elizabeth, Countess of Southampton. "My friend," she wrote, "amuses himself by devising a new coat of arms, in which the new town at Virginia will be prominent."

It was not to be, and the Crown did not extend to Smith the honor he deserved. He had to be content with only the title of former President of the Jamestown council. It was resounding enough, but unfortunately it meant nothing to most people, who had no idea of the structure of the early Jamestown colony. When Smith published his next book, in 1612, he rectified the situation by calling himself the former Governor of Virginia, which was at least correct in spirit if not in fact.

During the summer of 1610 Smith appeared, on numerous occasions, in the public company of the Prince of Wales, and on several others with the Earl and Countess of Southampton. For a period of at least a week he visited Sir Ferdinando's estate in the west of England. He seemed confident that his contributions to the cause of colonization would be soon recognized and would bring him the fame he desired. Late in the summer he paid a visit to the city of Plymouth, where Sir Ferdinando was governor, but in September he suddenly disappeared completely from public view.

There are no records of his activities for most of the next year. The Duchess of Richmond indicates in her correspondence that Smith continued to see her occasionally. Early in the winter months of 1611 she was annoyed because of his apparent interest in another woman, but no known liaison came from the presumed infatuation.

This is the only mention of him. He vanished from

164

London, mysteriously, giving up his lodgings. He did not visit his childhood home; both his sister and brother continued to write to ask him to visit after their long separation, hopefully in the near future.

It seems possible that he went to one of Southampton's estates for a long period of rest, or similarly that he went to a farm at the outskirts of Plymouth belonging to Sir Ferdinando. No one was upset by his disappearance or by his absence from London.

In the early summer of 1611 Smith returned to the city, much refreshed and in better health. He found a new apartment for himself right away, far more modest than his previous one. He then went to George Hall, his printer, for an accounting, and was pleased to learn that *A True Relation* was still selling well and that it had earned him another 780 pounds.

Smith had news of his own for Hall. The printer was delighted to hear that Smith was in the last stages of composition on a new book. This was *A Map of Virginia with a Description of the Country*, in which Smith planned to include the observations and accounts of other colonists who had been at Jamestown with him. He intended to call this section *The Proceedings of the English Colony in Virginia*. Percy had now returned to England and had written his own history of Jamestown for inclusion in this section, John Martin had added some pertinent comments, and John Russell had prepared a short essay. Other men who had backed Smith in Virginia also prepared letters and material for the forthcoming book.

Smith had his material ready for Hall by the autumn of 1611. Hall, however, was oddly reluctant to accept this new business, an attitude that was puzzling in view of the continuing success of *A True Relation*. When Smith pressed him, Hall finally said that he could not publish the book.

Smith did not need his great imaginative talent to figure out that someone in a high place opposed publication of his book. The most probable reason would be that it dealt bluntly and honestly with the problems of colonial living. Smith naturally suspected some of the directors of the London Company who had given him so much trouble in the past, but they refused to discuss the subject. Smith undertook a long investigation and eventually discovered a most unlikely enemy.

His opponent was Robert Carr, the younger son of a Scots noble, a young man of great charm and physical beauty but no apparant talents. He had been a page accompanying King James to England and had been very high in the royal favor. He had fallen from grace, then recently had once again become the favorite of the King. He was handsome, arrogant, and affected; he dressed with great elegance, at the height of male fashion. It was widely believed that his relationship with the King had passed the bounds of simple friendship.

Only a few months earlier Carr had been made a viscount and was now known as Lord Rochester. Within a short time he would be made a member of the Privy Council and private secretary to the King, and in less than two years he was to climb even higher, becoming the Earl of Somerset.

Lord Rochester had chosen, or been persuaded, to invest an enormous sum of money in the London Company. Unfortunately for Smith, he was an incurable dreamer who was still convinced that colonization of the New World was a path to easy wealth, and would rapidly repay him with large quantities of gold, diamonds, and other precious gems. When he read *A Map of Virginia* he was horrified by Smith's realistic appraisal and discussion of Jamestown affairs. He was certain the book would discourage colonization, and thus cost him a fortune. He had no trouble in convincing several of the other directors to accept his views.

Hall had been summoned to Rochester's elegant suite at Whitehall. Once there, the printer had been informed that if he published Smith's book he would receive no further printing orders from the Crown. Hall depended on Crown business for a significant part of his income, as did every other publisher, so he had no choice but to reject publication of *A Map of Virginia.*

Smith had no intention of tamely giving up, but when he appealed to his powerful friends for help he found them unwilling to become involved in a dispute with the King's favorite. Sir Ferdinando had to be especially careful, for he had earned the displeasure of King James several years earlier. Southampton would have loved nothing more than to fight on behalf of his friend, being of an aggressive disposition, but his Countess persuaded him that to earn the wrath of the King would be foolhardy.

Smith's most powerful potential ally was Prince Henry, who could have swept aside the opposition of even Rochester. The Prince of Wales had fallen ill, however, and was seeing no one. So grave was his illness that in a few short months he would be dead. Smith sent two letters to the Prince but did not receive an answer to either. It is possible that Henry did not even receive them, surrounded as he was by courtiers of his father.

It seemed that Smith must fail in his efforts, but he persevered. He knew his book was worthy of publication, and what was even more important, he knew the cause of colonization would suffer if prospective settlers were deceived and the wrong sort of colonist went to the New World. Only the truth would bring the right kind of settler to cross the ocean to settle permanently in the wilderness.

In the spring of 1612 *A Map of Virginia* was published, suddenly and unexpectedly, in Oxford. Although the edition bore the name of no printer, it was obvious that someone at the famous university, one of several men who printed books for the students, had done the job and had remained discreetly anonymous. It was also obvious that significant influence must have been brought to bear within the academic community to ensure publication.

No one really really doubted that the influence was Richard Hakluyt's. The great geographer was afraid of no one, neither the King nor his current favorite, and he had deep and close relations with the university. But if the Archdeacon were responsible he kept quiet about it. And so did Smith, who would not compromise his benefactor. No correspondence between them on the subject has ever been discovered, so it is only reasonable guesswork and probability that point to Hakluyt as the man responsible for publication of *A Map of Virginia*. The scholar would have wanted the book published as it would be of great value to colonial planners and settlers alike.

Rochester was naturally furious. He and his friends tried to persuade King James, through the agency of the Privy Council, to have the book withdrawn. James hesitated, for despite his obvious faults he was an essentially fair man, and a better judge of character than most people believed. Elizabeth of Southampton wrote to

168

Frances, Duchess of Richmond, that the King had a copy of *A Map of Virginia* and might possibly even have read some of it.

In any case, the King refused to have the book banned. It contained nothing seditious, and he could see no reason to withdraw it. Even if Smith were jeopardizing some large colonial investments, he had spent several years in Virginia and could be presumed to know what he was talking about. Furthermore, detailed reports sent from Jamestown by Lord De La Warr indicated in great detail that many of Smith's ideas were sound. The King felt that Smith had the right, like any other Englishman, to express his ideas in print.

Rochester, annoyed when the book was not withdrawn, went on to make a big mistake. He tried to threaten the London booksellers, but he could threaten them only with a loss of his patronage, which was not very great. It was a foolish thing to do, and word spread rapidly. The effect of Rochester's actions was to increase the popularity of *A Map of Virginia*, stimulating those who might have been otherwise indifferent to go out and buy the book. Most of the literate populace was now eager to read it, if only to see what all the fuss was about.

The book was an immediate success. The initial modest printing was sold out in a few days, and the two following printings, much larger, sold out in six months. As a result, interest in *A True Relation* was rekindled, and sales of that book picked up again also. George Hall was placed in the pleasantly embarrassing position of having to bring out a new edition of that work.

By the autumn of 1612 Prince Henry, Smith's patron, was dead, and Smith knew he would never be received at court or rewarded by the Crown, due to the influence

169

of Lord Rochester. But despite all the royal snubs, Smith was a man of consequence, enjoying respect and admiration.

Merchants interested in expanding their markets into the New World, and nobles thinking of investing in or forming new companies for exploration and trade, eagerly asked Smith for advice. They not only asked him for it, they paid him for it. Everyone with an interest in the New World seemed to want his guidance. The country was alive with excitement, thinking and talking of discovery and colonization, wanting to capitalize on new opportunities. The exploits of Henry Hudson added fuel to the fire. When Hudson returned to England after finding what would later become the site of New York City, he thanked Smith publicly for his assistance, and praised him. This gave an added boost to Smith's reputation.

Now that Smith had the fame he had craved he no longer reacted to it. When strangers sought to speak to him on the streets, or when he was pointed out in taverns, he was neither bothered nor excessively flattered. He had gained maturity, and had learned that an increase in responsibility went with an increase in stature. Although he still enjoyed recognition, he was more concerned with the establishment of successful and flourishing colonies. The New World was his passion.

He remained unchanged in several vital respects, however. When anyone came to him for advice, whether merchant, noble, or prospective emigrant, he told the plain truth about conditions in America. Sir Walter Raleigh advised Smith to take a different course. Sir Walter, still in the Tower, was trying to win his release with lies, promising the King he would find a fabulous gold mine for the Crown in Central America. Raleigh told Smith, who still visited him, that he was likely to end in prison also unless he told the King and the great nobles what they wanted to hear.

Smith would have none of it. Jamestown had made a permanent impression on him that went far deeper than the scars from his powder burns. He strongly believed that the New World was no place for idle adventure-seekers, but only for those willing to earn their living by hard and persistent labor.

Smith's vaunted integrity failed him in one important respect, however, nearly costing him a valuable friend and benefactor. His increased fame had made him much more attractive to women, and he took advantage of the situation to engage in brief affairs in 1612. There were two of them, one unimportant. The other almost lost him the friendship of the Duchess of Richmond.

The woman in question was little more than a girl. Margaret Wriothesley, only seventeen years old, was a cousin of the Earl of Southampton and a great beauty, a blonde in the mold of Smith's beloved mother. She had not yet been presented at Whitehall, where, it was expected, a suitable marriage would be arranged for her. She seriously damaged her chances for such a marriage by associating with Smith. According to customs of the age, no one would have cared if she waited until after marriage to have an affair, or as many as she liked, but to do so beforehand was to court disaster.

The Duchess of Richmond was furious with her friend, the Countess of Southampton, whom she quaintly accused of encouraging the liaison. She was understandably even angrier with Smith. She did not expect fidelity of her husband; no one did. But she ex-

171

pected it of her official lover. Smith hastily terminated his relationship with Margaret.

Margaret returned to her parents in Sussex, where she remained until the gossip had died down and she was once again considered eligible. But Smith's situation was a little more difficult. Frances had closed her door to him, and he was deprived of her help in the realm of high society.

After Frances ignored two letters of apology Smith sent her, he resorted to a gesture that in later times appears farcical: he asked her husband to intervene on his behalf. But the Duchess ignored this, too. Smith had gravely insulted her by having a relationship not with a commoner, but with another aristocrat. Smith eventually resolved the ludicrous situation by giving her a ruby ring set in gold. Frances accepted the gift, and peace was made.

 **24**

That the Jamestown experiment was a success was obvious by 1613 to anyone interested in the progress of English colonization. England would not be outdistanced in the rush to acquire New World lands. Lord De La Warr had restored order to the Virginia colony by following the example Smith had set and by enforcing the principles of self-support and discipline. The directors of the London Company had been guaranteed a steady, if modest, return on their investment, and other companies were being formed, with the London Company for a model, to explore and colonize new lands.

Smith kept himself informed of developments in Jamestown, but despite his possessive interest he knew he had no place in the colony's future; his contributions were now history. He took care to make it plain to his former superiors that he was willing to return to Jamestown, overlooking all former slights, if a suitable position could be found for him in the colony. No appropriate place could be found, however—not because there was no such position, but because Smith insisted on bluntly speaking the truth with no regard for its effect on the less practical plans of others. This attitude, combined with his fierce independence, had made him too many enemies, and by 1613 he realized that he had no future in Virginia.

Although he accepted the fact that he could not return to Jamestown he longed desperately to return to the wilderness. He was afraid that another man might eclipse his achievements in the New World, and he knew that his own experience made him eminently qualified to lead an expedition, either for exploration, discovery, or settlement. He began to think of the New World as his own personal domain.

Smith probably had more firsthand knowledge of the New World than any other man in England at the time. He not only knew something of the native inhabitants and their languages and customs, but he had sailed up rivers and marched across hundreds of miles of forests. He could not rest comfortably in London while other men went back to his continent and made history.

The fervor of interest in the New World served him well. The attention of English investors was not confined to Virginia alone, and Smith was qualified to lead an expedition into other regions. In particular, Smith's attention turned to the area then known as the northern part of Virginia, which he was later to name New England.

Over the past eleven years some information had been gleaned about that area. The first of the early voyages had been commanded by Captain Bartholomew Gosnold, Smith's companion at Jamestown. Gosnold, sailing in the *Concord* and financed by the Earl of Southampton, had investigated the natural riches of New England, establishing temporary headquarters on what was probably Martha's Vineyard. He bartered with natives who canoed over from the mainland, filling his hold with American merchandise including cedar and sassafras. Before some unfortunate incidents with the Indians forced him to leave, he had determined to his satisfaction that the region was a "paradise," with one of the most healthful climates on the continent. It must be remembered that Gosnold was in the region only during the spring and early summer; he did not experience a New England winter.

When Gosnold returned to England he had only extravagant praise for the "goodliest continent that ever we saw." He told Hakluyt of his voyage, and a steady stream of descriptions kept flowing to the English public. Smith, in 1613, still possessed all of Gosnold's notes and charts, which were unfortunately far from complete.

So intrigued was Hakluyt with Gosnold's discoveries that in 1603 the Archdeacon persuaded the wealthy citizens of Bristol to finance another expedition. It accomplished little, and in 1605 was followed by an expedition lead by Captain George Waymouth. He indulged in some brazen kidnapping among the coastal tribes, which laid a foundation of mistrust for later settlers. Waymouth's charts contradicted Gosnold's in hundreds of details, but his Indian captives proved wonderful propagandists. They had learned English rapidly, and they knew their only chance of getting home again lay in the increased desirability of future voyages to their land. They spread tales of gold mines and lucrative commerce with China.

The would-be promoters needed no such encouragement. There were constant disputes over which group held what rights to which half-charted territories. In

1606 King James had to take action to eliminate these domestic rivalries. Investors based in London were granted rights in North America from Maryland to Georgia, while the vast north was reserved for promoters from cities like Exeter, Bristol, Plymouth, and Newport, in southwestern England.

Two of the men with rights in this part of North America were Smith's close friends and supporters, Sir Ferdinando and the Earl of Southampton. The Earl dispatched another expedition to the area in 1607, but the gain from the voyage did not justify the tremendous investment. Captain Edward Harlow, in command of this voyage, brought back word that the area that would eventually be called Cape Cod was not an island, as had previously been supposed, but was part of the mainland. Harlow had also kidnapped natives, who were shipped to England and exhibited for money. One of them convinced Sir Ferdinando that his homeland was gold-rich. Sir Ferdinando promptly sent him back home as a guide with Captain Thomas Hobson. Once back in New England, the native lost no time in trying to murder Hobson and his crew, before escaping inland. This voyage also had a notable lack of success.

Sir John Popham, the Lord Chief Justice, financed another expedition, intending to set up a colony that was actually to be a sister settlement to Jamestown. Some of Waymouth's captives had convinced him that there were gold mines in the area. Perhaps this is one reason for Popham's refusal to believe Smith about the absence of precious metals in North America; the natives, after all, had told him there was gold.

There was no gold. The Indian interpreter-guides, after promising to contact their tribes and then return to the ships, completely disappeared, and the pioneers were inexperienced in wilderness living. Jamestown's might-have-been sister colony failed.

It was into this breach that Smith decided to step. He wanted to make a voyage with the specific purpose of obtaining accurate information about the area to the north of Hudson's river. He sent a letter to the Earl of Southampton in which he proposed that he make the journey to accurately map the coastline and to explore "such portions of the interior as may seem worthy of discovery."

Both the Earl of Southampton and Sir Ferdinando encouraged him, and Hakluyt made available all the information that he had. Smith then retired to Plymouth, to one of Sir Ferdinando's estates, to study the situation in peace and quiet.

Smith was struck by one fact that seemed particularly significant to him: the abundance of whales. Henry Hudson, before his famous westward voyage, had twice looked for an Arctic passage to the Pacific on behalf of his investors, the Muscovy Company. At the island later to be known as Spitsbergen he had found a huge school of whales, initiating a race between fishermen of various countries including England, France, Holland, and Spain.

Whale oil had an enormous commercial value, and ambergris, a whale product, was much sought after for making perfume. Spitsbergen was now the site of several boom towns, and various national governments were giving their fishermen not only financial aid but naval protection.

Smith thought it strange that although every expedition across the Atlantic in northern waters had reported large numbers of whales off the American coast, the fishing industry had not yet reacted to the news. There was no commercial race for whales in American waters. From Gosnold's notes, still in his possession, and from Waymouth's logs, which he borrowed from Hakluyt, he knew there were large schools of cod and tuna in the same waters. In the back of his mind was the remembrance of the fortunate tuna catch that had saved Jamestown from starvation.

Smith had a simple but brilliant idea that had not occurred to anyone else: he would equip his expedition in a novel way. Harpoons for taking whales, heavy nets for catching cod and tuna, and empty kegs and a large supply of salt could help the expedition earn far more than its own way. For once the investors would have hope of an immediate return on their investment. His voyage, ideally, would show a profit on the day the ships returned to England.

 **25**

Smith set about planning for his voyage with great care. He thought it reasonable that someone who had experience dealing with the natives would be able to barter capably for furs. He politely informed his investors that he intended to look for gold and copper mines, but that he would take on, as a last resort, fish and furs. He knew full well that fish and furs, far from being a last resort, would be primary cargo.

He wanted to leave as little to chance as possible, and with this in mind he sought out two Indians who had been brought back by Waymouth's expedition. Smith spent many days with them, trying to learn their language. His familiarity with the Virginia dialects enabled him to learn with relative ease, for this northern language was related to those he knew. The two natives became friendly with him, telling him in great detail about their homeland, and Smith was careful to take extensive notes on all they said. No one else had been interested enough to do this since the Indians arrived in England.

The two natives were of a different physical type than the Chickahominy Smith had known. They were more slender, of slighter build, with darker, deep-copper skins. Both were young, in their late twenties or early thirties. Smith knew they would be valuable guides in the North American wilderness, and he made them the offer they had been hoping for: he would give them passage back to their homes if they would promise to act as his guides once they reached their own country. Naturally they leaped at the chance.

Smith kept his word and took the two Indians back to New England. There is reason to believe that this action may have given rise to one of the most astonishing, and important, incidents in the history of British colonization of North America.

Smith left the Indians at a place he called, and marked on the map, New Plymouth. One of them apparently died soon thereafter of a sickness contracted in England, but the other survived. He was there, six years later, when a small band of English settlers came ashore from the ship *Mayflower*. The Pilgrims probably would not have survived without Squanto's help.

This tale may not be quite as straightforward as it seems. It is possible that Squanto did not reach England until 1614, as a captive of Thomas Hunt, whom Sir Ferdinando called "a worthless fellow of our nation," and that he eventually worked for the Newfoundland Company, not the merchants who backed Smith. This version would have it that Squanto made several journeys back to his home with his friend, Captain Thomas Dermer. When Dermer died he returned to his homeland only to find that his subtribe, the Patuxet band of the Wampanoags, had been exterminated by a plague the European sailors had introduced. He joined another band, and was on hand to aid the Pilgrims. But Sir Ferdinando mentions Squanto as one of the Indians brought back by Waymouth, and the tangled evidence makes it impossible to be certain. It is difficult to believe that Sir Ferdinando would have been mistaken about the identity of someone so important, and Smith did return two Indians to their homes, so it is at least possible that Squanto was one of them.

In any event, Smith continued to plan with extraordinary care, determined to make his voyage a success. He had learned from Hudson's experiences that it was better to make a voyage with a small crew to keep expenses low. He wanted two ships, however, each one hundred tons, with large holds to store the oil, fish, and furs that were expected to pay for the expedition.

Smith received Hakluyt's immediate support, and Hakluyt was able to obtain financing for him almost overnight, such was his influence. The Duke of Richmond was one of the three most influential men who supplied funds for the voyage. Smith was therefore able to ignore ordinary discretion and name his flagship the *Frances*. The major portion of the rest of the money Smith needed was provided by Southampton and Sir Ferdinando, who had backed so many other enterprises of exploration. They both guaranteed Smith a free hand in outfitting, staffing, and directing his expedition.

The first thing Smith did was to hire two veteran and expert seamen. One was Captain George Langam, who had sailed with Waymouth but was nonetheless known as a man of excellent personal character. He was ruddy of complexion but taciturn, especially in comparison with Captain Marmaduke Royden, who was a cheerful extrovert endowed with a thick red beard, a booming voice, and a jolly manner that won him almost instant confidence. He had been the second mate under the famed explorer John Davys, and thus had been a shipmate of Hudson's. Smith, whose only mistake in character judgment had been in regard to Matthew Scrivener, was certain that Royden was just the sort of mariner he wanted.

Smith permitted Langam and Royden to choose their own crews, but he retained the power of veto over their choices. He sat with them when they conducted their interviews and checked the lists of those they wished to sign on, but he used his veto power sparingly.

Smith also hired two former professional soldiers, William Skelton and John Buley. They were expert swordsmen and marksmen, but otherwise little is known of them. Smith knew from his experience at Jamestown that gentlemen-adventurers could be valuable assistants on shore, and he was obviously satisfied with these two.

Preparations for the voyage were stepped up toward the end of 1613. Smith had purchased his flagship, the *Frances*, a ship of 105 tons, and he gave her to Langam. Very shortly afterwards he purchased a ship of eighty-two tons. Royden insisted that this was, in reality, the better ship, and events later proved him right; she was easier to handle in rough weather. Smith tactfully named her the *Queen Anne*.

The two captains, with the aid of the two gentlemen-adventurers, bought the provisions and all the equipment for the voyage. Smith personally examined everything, from kegs of meat and fish to barrels of flour; he remembered that merchants were only too anxious to pass off their inferior merchandise on those who did not know what to look for. He was determined that his expedition would not be supplied with lumpy gunpowder, spoiled food, or weevil-infested biscuits.

Smith had the ships outfitted at Southampton, where there were extensive wharves and warehouses belonging to the Earl. In early February the crews were brought aboard, but Smith continued to live for about ten more days in a town house the Earl of Southampton had made available to him. Eventually he had his gear brought aboard the *Frances*, on which the two Indians, Skelton, and Buley were also to sail. Smith had a private cabin with a bunk and a ledge that could serve as a table for writing, if he used a sea chest for a chair. Such accommodations were luxurious on this type of vessel.

The sailing was delayed by bad weather, a happening that must have seemed unfortunately familiar to Smith. Early in the morning of March 3, 1614, the sun finally came out and the seas calmed, allowing the two little ships to leave and head out into the English Channel. Smith's entire company for both ships, including the two Indians, the gentlemen-adventurers, two physicians (one for each ship), and two cabin boys, came to only forty-five persons. He had managed to keep the size of his crews to a minimum.

The long voyage across the Atlantic was made completely without incident, so well did Smith's crews function, and so well had he planned. Although the ships were separated for three days by a storm, they found each other again with no problem. For a while there was brief excitement when they thought they had sighted an island, but it turned out to be only an iceberg. Smith wrote gravely, in his book *A Description of New England*, that he and several others of the crew of the *Frances* had seen a mermaid sitting on the iceberg. His readers did not find this especially unusual; many mermaids were sighted in the seventeenth century. Hudson also claimed

183

to have seen one of the watery ladies on one of his voyages. Although many explanations have been advanced as to what sort of animal the mariners really did see, the delusion of mermaids was a common one.

By the middle of April the two ships had reached the Grand Banks of Newfoundland. The fish were so plentiful in these waters that the men spent hours staring over the sides in wonder at them. But Smith did not engage in much fishing. He ordered his captains to proceed down the coast in search of whales. Two days later they did indeed sight whales, and all hands were set to work in pursuit of a possible fortune.

Sighting one of the huge mammals and killing it are two very different propositions, however. Smith found that his harpoons were not sturdy enough to penetrate the skin of the whales, and once the whales realized they were hunted, they were remarkably speedy in escaping. Smith continued to chase them for another twenty-four hours, but his ships could not match their speed. Finally he gave up and decided, more practically, to concentrate on fishing. Royden, with perhaps a touch of sour grapes, determined that the whales were of the wrong breed anyway; he did not think they carried ambergris or useful oil.

By now the ships were off the coast of what would become known as Nova Scotia. It was here that Smith developed a technique he would continue to use while he was in the New World. There were seven small boats on board the *Frances* and the _Queen Anne_. They had been built in sections and lashed to the decks. Now they were put together by ships' carpenters, and Smith declared that six of them were to be used for fishing. Smith took the remaining boat himself. Accompanied by the Indians, the gentlemen-adventurers, and three crewman, he rowed as close to shore as he could. There he began to draw maps and charts that he hoped would include the coastline of the whole region.

The fishing was excellent. They caught more fish than they could use or store. Everyone ate well, and all the empty barrels in the hold were filled with fish oil, dried tuna and salted codfish. Smith estimated their catch at approximately fifty thousand fish from mid-April, when they first approached the American mainland, to mid-July, when they began their voyage back to England.

Smith had even greater success than the taking of so many fish. His maps of the coastline were surprisingly accurate, and he mapped all the way from Nova Scotia and New Brunswick to Rhode Island. He charted the mouths of Maine's great rivers, the Kennebec and the Penobscot, and went ashore at the site of what would become Portsmouth, New Hampshire. In this area, with the help of the two Indians, he engaged in trade with some of the local sachems. In marked contrast with the behavior of the preceding English explorers along the coast, his relations with the Indians were amicable. In fact, Smith did much to offset the damage done by Waymouth, Harlow, and Hunt, and to mitigate their unsavory legacy. He exchanged mirrors, beads, and other trinkets for several bales of fine furs.

The weather was fine, and now that friendly relations with the natives had been established, he spent most of his time ashore, beginning on April 30. In Massachusetts he discovered the Merrimack River and traveled up it for a short distance. He spent two days near the site of what would be Boston with the Massachusetts Indians. He traded for more furs, and promised to return the next year to aid them against their enemies. He was not able to keep his promise, however, and the Massachusetts were destroyed eventually—not by human enemies but by a European epidemic, probably smallpox. Smith named the river in the area the Charles, after the surviving son of King James, who would later become Charles I.

Smith released the two natives, as he had promised, near their homes, at the place he named New Plymouth. He found the waters around the sandy peninsula of Cape Cod, the region discovered by Bartholomew Gosnold in 1602, to be teeming with fish.

Smith then sailed southward and entered the waters of Rhode Island's huge Narragansett Bay. Excitement mounted as Smith considered the possibility that this might be the Pacific passage. When this idea proved untenable, he still thought for a time that it might be the estuary of an enormous river, but he finally satisfied himself that it was not. He continued his policy of trading with the Indians for furs, and of course he continued with his painstaking mapmaking.

Smith later wrote, "I carried with me six large charts of these localities, each so unlike another and most so differing from any true proportion or resemblance of the Country, that they did me no more good than so much waste paper, though they cost me more." He tried, by his efforts, to right this situation.

He was quite modest about his contributions, however. As he said in *A Description of New England:* "I have drawn a Map from Point to Point, Isle to Isle and Harbor to Harbor, with the soundings, sands, rocks, and landmarks as I passed close aboard the shore in a little boat, although there be many things to be observed which the haste of other affairs did cause me to omit. For being sent more to get present commodities than knowledge by discovery for future good, I had not power to search as I would. Thus you may see, of this two thousand miles of New World coastal lands, more than half is unknown to any purpose."

Despite his reservations and unhappiness at not being permitted more time for discovery and exploration, Smith made the first complete map of the area. Like his other maps, it was astonishingly accurate. The voyage had also been a financial success, and Smith knew it; his careful plans had paid off. The holds and decks of his ships were stocked almost to overflowing with barrels of fish oil, salted and dried fish, and large bundles of the magnificent New World furs. With all this completed, Smith set sail for home on July 18.

The return voyage was calm, pleasant, and quick. Smith reached London at the end of August. The whole expedition had been a short one; from beginning to end it had lasted less than six months. Within twenty-four hours of docking the entire cargo had been sold. The investors paid off all their expenses, including the wages of the crews, and even the cost of the ships themselves, and found that they had a profit of an astonishing eight thousand pounds. Out of this they gave Smith fifteen hundred pounds, enough to let him live comfortably for several years.

His success made quite a stir among merchants and others interested in the New World. Smith had known, since he first went to Jamestown, that the profits of the New World were not to be found in gold, silver, and diamonds, but in furs, lumber, fish, and in the value of the colonies themselves. Finally, over seven years after the start of the Jamestown experiment, it dawned on investors that those natural resources that the new continent could offer were just as valuable as gold and precious gems.

Smith initially paid no attention to the excitement he was creating in financial circles. He retired immediately to a farm outside the city of Plymouth that belonged to Sir Ferdinando and went right to work completing the maps he made in the waters of the New World and filling in the details. He gave the original of his master map to Charles, the new Prince of Wales, and politely suggested that he change any of the place names he did not like.

Charles made only two major changes. He changed Cape Cod to Cape James, after his father; but Smith's original name stuck, and in common usage Charles's preference was ignored. One name was permanently changed. Cape Tragabigzanda, which Smith had named after his Turkish mistress, was too difficult for the English to swallow, let alone pronounce. The Prince changed the name of the cape to honor his mother and called it Cape Ann. He did not alter the name Smith had given some shoals off the New Hampshire coast. Smith had named them Smith's Isles.

Richard Hakluyt was pleased with Smith's superb maps, and the geographers of Oxford and Cambridge were equally delighted. Smith had great hopes of at last receiving academic honors, but the professors had to give more thought to the matter. Smith thereupon returned to London to make a triumphal tour of his favorite taverns. For this purpose he chose to wear a beautiful cape of fox fur draped over his light armor, disregarding the fact that it was summer.

Smith found himself immensely popular. Eager investors wined and dined him and squabbled over the honor of escorting him around London. Attractive women fawned over him, and Smith cheerfully hinted of the attentions of several belles in his letter to Sir Ferdinando, but he rejected their attentions. Frances was also in London, and they were seen openly in one another's company.

Smith lost his chance for academic honors in the autumn of 1614. He was so starved for praise, or so overcome with his own accomplishments, that he made a spectacle of himself by bragging in taverns, and the academicians promptly canceled their offers asking him to lecture at Oxford or Cambridge, or to meet with the faculties there. Smith was behaving in a manner far too flamboyant to win the approval of the staid and conservative dons. Smith might have been a gentleman, but he was not, in their opinion, acting like one. Although they were quick to adopt the name he had given the new territory he had mapped, New England, and to recognize his many other accomplishments, they chose to pretend he did not exist.

Merchants and nobles who wished to invest in the New World were less fussy. Even Lord Rochester, who had just been made Earl of Somerset, went out of his way to treat Smith with consideration. People may have laughed at Smith's affected manner and his flashy fox cape, but they also realized the high price those same furs would bring on the London market.

Smith made the most of his sudden success. Investors plagued him for the chance to become partners or backers in his next expedition. So eager were they to enlist his services, and only his, that they offered him any terms he pleased. Although Smith was flattered, he was not tempted; in business matters, at least, he retained a clear head. He remained loyal to his old friends, Sir Ferdinando, Southampton, and Richmond, who had aided him when no one else had been willing to believe in him. He announced that he would undertake expeditions for no other investors.

In this manner he finally gained a little peace as would-be backers stopped pestering him. He was at last able to devote his attention to planning another expedition, which was to be the most ambitious of all his projects. He wanted to establish a colony in New England and to support it solely with the profits made from furs and fish and lumber. A few selected settlers would make the initial trip to the site of the colony, preparing it for others who would follow later.

As Smith planned the venture, the investors would be required to lay out very little money. The profits from the colony would be plowed back into the venture at the outset, keeping intial costs low. If it were managed judiciously, he believed, the New England settlement could be self-supporting almost from the beginning.

Some new investors were admitted to the ranks of Smith's supporters on the previous voyage. They were all from western England, and among them was the Dean of Exeter. But as the number of investors increased, so did the friction. Smith's primary objective was to establish a colony, but theirs was immediate profit, which they now knew could be gained from fishing. Smith was adamant—and arrogant—and he insisted on making his own plans.

By March 1615 the new expedition was ready. Smith had two ships which his backers had bought. One was a magnificent vessel weighing two hundred tons. The smaller was a rather more battered vessel weighing only fifty tons. Forty-four settlers had been hand-picked by Smith from hundreds of applicants, and this time he was sure that he had colonists of the caliber he wanted, earnest people who were willing to work hard. The entire company numbered only ninety-four persons, the other fifty being sailors and fishermen.

Smith continued his practice of personally checking the supplies for the expedition, making sure that the food was unspoiled and the gunpowder of good quality. He was going to be the first governor of New England, and he was not about to let inattention to any detail, no matter how minor, ruin his glowing future.

The departure of the expedition from Plymouth was quiet, lacking in the drama that might ordinarily be expected from Smith. He had been so busy that he was unable to visit London before sailing, and had written rather casually to Frances, Duchess of Richmond, that he would be away from England "for a half-decade, mayhap, or a trifle longer."

All of Smith's careful plans were upset. A furious gale blew across the Atlantic from the west, striking the two ships when they were only 350 miles from England. The masts on the large ship broke, and she began to leak so badly that the crew had to pump in shifts to keep her afloat. They managed to patch her up, but Smith knew the repairs were not good enough to get them safely to America. There was only one decision that could be made under the circumstances: Smith gave the order to turn back.

After a voyage of only three and a half weeks, the two battered ships returned to Plymouth. Most of the settlers had been so ill on their unlucky voyage that they changed their minds about colonization and backed out. The two-hundred-ton ship could not be repaired, and the investors began demanding that their money be returned. Smith struggled desperately to start again.

 **26**

Smith's dream of founding a colony faded swiftly. He could obtain no more money from his investors until their previous investment paid off, and Smith did not see how this could be done. His flagship was a derelict, and his settlers had decided to do their settling in England, after all. Smith realized that if he wanted to sail at all, he would have to revise his plans drastically. He could not find a replacement for his two-hundred-ton flagship, and he had to recruit new settlers. He decided to buy time.

The first step was to send off the fifty-ton ship on a fishing expedition to the New World. He knew that if the voyage were successful, as he fully expected it to be in those rich waters, he could repay at least a significant part of his deficit. He then proceeded to sell what he could from the wreckage of his flagship, including all the equipment he had intended to use in establishing his colony. He got a good price for the muskets, and also for the two cannon he had planned to locate in his fort.

With the money he accumulated from these sales he was able to purchase a sixty-ton merchantman, and he stocked it with provisions he had kept for just this purpose. He rehired twenty-three of the best seamen from the crew of his former flagship, then started out again to fish in New England waters. To further keep down expenses, he acted as his own ship's master, for the first and last time in his career.

Smith sailed late in June. He was only ten days out of Plymouth when he was sighted by a much larger ship. Smith's vessel fled, but the other ship continued the chase for forty-eight hours. The larger ship was faster, and also carried cannon. Smith gave up his attempt to escape after two shots across the bow.

When the privateer drew alongside, Smith was astonished to find that her master was a man named Fry, with whom he had served in Transylvania. Fry's first mate Chambers had also been an officer in the same battalion. At this point history becomes stranger than fiction. Smith persuaded Fry to go to New England with him, and the two ships headed west together. Smith had increased the size of his expedition.

Less than one week later, in mid-Atlantic, they ran across bad luck. It came in the form of four ships, the largest about 160 tons. Smith and Fry hoisted the British flag, but the strangers continued to bear down on them. When they were close enough they opened fire, but so abruptly that the English had no warning, and two of Fry's cannon were put out of action. The attackers then raised the banner of France. As England and France were currently at peace, it was obvious that the Frenchmen were pirates.

Although the two English ships were helpless, Smith still hoped to be able to talk his way out of the situation. With this in mind he had himself rowed over to the French flagship, the *Sauvage*, and was conducted to the commodore's cabin. This turned out to be an elegant ruffian named d'Elbert, who had no known scruples. While he and Smith talked, he sent prize crews to take command of the two English ships. Smith was not allowed to return to his ship, but was kept as a prisoner on the *Sauvage*.

Although helpless, Smith was desperate to win freedom for himself, his crew, and his ship. He badly needed to get to New England waters to obtain the tuna, cod, and furs that could be sold in London to finance his colony. He tried continually to persuade d'Elbert to release him, but the pirate was only amused at his prisoner's desperate promises of future wealth in return for immediate release.

The four French ships and the two English vessels now made up a small squadron, and they sailed southward into the shipping lanes used by the Spaniards in their South American traffic. Smith had to spend his nights under guard in the gunroom of the *Sauvage*, but his days were of necessity spent on deck, because ammunition was stored in his prison.

In the hope of winning the confidence of d'Elbert by a different approach, Smith helped devise tactics that enabled the French pirate to capture three Spanish ships within two weeks. He did convince d'Elbert that he knew a great deal about battle tactics at sea, but the Frenchman still refused his continued requests for release.

There were now nine ships in the squadron, with thinly spread French crews trying to manage them all. The English seamen on Smith's and Fry's vessels took advantage of this fact and managed to overwhelm their captors one dark night, sailing off before they were discovered. In fact, their absence was not discovered until the following morning. Had Smith not been held on d'Elbert's ship, he too would have made good his escape. Both ships reached England safely, where they made a full report of their capture and escape to a Royal Admiralty commission. Smith was presumed dead and was duly mourned by his friends.

But Smith was still very much alive. He remained a prisoner on the French vessel while the privateers roamed the Atlantic. He was forced to watch on one occasion when a Scottish ship bound for Bristol with a load of sugar from the West Indies was captured and sunk.

During one fight a courageous Portuguese sloop-of-war was taken as a prize, but not before d'Elbert was mortally wounded. His position as commodore was assumed by the master of the *Sauvage*, a huge man named Poyrune. Where d'Elbert had been crafty, Poyrune was ruthless, and insatiably greedy as well. He transferred all the loot he could from other vessels to his own.

The end result of this action was that the other ships deserted him, one by one, unwilling to serve such an unreasonable man. He still continued on his own, however, raiding, burning and sinking merchantmen wherever he found them on the high seas. Odd as it may seem, Smith's lot actually improved after Poyrune assumed command. Although the new commodore was reluctant to release someone who knew so much about his operations, he saw nothing to be gained by keeping Smith constantly under guard. There was, after all, no longer any way for him to escape. Smith was therefore allowed to move his mattress to the "great cabin" of the *Sauvage*, and when the ship was not actually engaged in attacking a merchantman, he was allowed to roam freely around the ship.

Smith remained as an unwilling guest of the pirates from August to October 1615, sailing the Atlantic with them. He was depressed, bored, and restless. Eventually, because he had nothing else to do, he began work on a new book. This was the beginning of *A Description of New England,* and Smith wrote in detail about his voyage of the preceding year. The book was destined not only to enjoy an enormous sale in England, but to arouse such interest in foreign countries that it would be translated into Dutch, French, and German. It is remarkable that its calm style and smooth flow of narrative do not reflect in any way Smith's emotional suffering at the time of its writing.

By this time the Frenchmen, some of whom were acting as crews for newly captured prize vessels, had been at sea for a long time. Poyrune was having an increasingly difficult time controlling them, and he knew that sooner or later he would have to let them go ashore. By late October there was no longer any real discipline on board, and he was forced to sail for France.

Poyrune's situation was difficult, as was that of his men. Smith's was no better. He knew he would be treated as a pirate by the French government if he were captured in the company of pirates. Although the British Admiralty courts had been lenient in their treatment of pirates since the days of Drake and Hawkins—provided, that is, the pirates had not attacked fellow Englishmen —the French took a much more severe view of the practice. Pirates were pirates, and if they were caught they were hanged.

Consequently Poyrune had to be extremely careful in making his plans. He eventually decided to sail to the seaport-fortress of La Rochelle, about one hundred miles southeast of Nantes. La Rochelle had many sailors who were active in fishing off the Newfoundland coasts, and Poyrune hoped to be able to pass his ships off as recently returned fishermen from the New World, if it should prove necessary.

He hoped it would not be necessary, for the disguise might wear thin. His preferred plan revolved around two bleak islands, Oléron and Ré, which stand at the entrance to La Rochelle's bay. They had become the headquarters of go-betweens who bought merchandise from the privateers, asking no embarrassing questions. Poyrune intended to sell his loot, which was worth more than one hundred thousand pounds, to the smugglers on the Ile de Ré.

The pirates reached France without mishap, but once there they were faced with a furious November gale. Poyrune was forced to seek shelter in a small cove on the Ile de Ré, fifteen miles from the larger harbor used by the smugglers. He intended to sit out the storm before making port as he had planned.

By this time Smith was desperate, willing to take almost any risk to escape from the pirates and afraid he might not have another chance. When everyone else on board the *Sauvage* went below for the night, Smith crept up to the rain-drenched deck with the nearly completed manuscript of *A Description of New England* stuffed safely under his shirt. With great difficulty, trying not to make noise, he managed to lower the ship's smallest boat into the water and to climb into it. He had with him a small knife, the only weapon he had been allowed to keep, and with this he cut himself adrift. He then tried to row to La Rochelle.

Smith, with no knowledge of the waters near La Rochelle, was caught in a crosscurrent that threatened to carry the little boat out to the open sea. Only a sudden change in the wind saved Smith from this fate. He rowed continuously, but the high seas made it necessary to pause frequently to bail the boat. Although Smith could see lights in the three great towers that guarded the port, he did not seem to be getting any closer to them.

The nightmare situation continued till nearly dawn. Only the change of the tide in the early morning saved Smith by sweeping him into the harbor. Exhausted and half-drowned, barely able to row the boat, he was sighted at last by a sentry in the Tower of St. Nicholas. A party of customs agents came out to meet him in a longboat.

An hour later, in the great hall of the tower, he told the Lord Lieutenant of the port the story of his escape. He considered the fact that he had escaped from the *Sauvage* in such weather and under such circumstances sufficient proof that he was not one of the pirates. While Smith revived himself with a breakfast of beef, cheese, and wine, an alarm was sounded, and every available ship in the harbor was sent to capture the pirates.

The storm had not been kind to Poyrune. Two of his ships had sunk during the night, and the other two had been badly damaged. When the pirates on the remaining ships saw the attackers approaching, they fled in small boats. The result was that they suffered even greater casualties. Some were shot, and some, among them Poyrune, were drowned after a boat capsized.

The French recovered about forty thousand pounds' worth of loot from the ships, which made Smith the hero

199

of La Rochelle, at that time a community of about fifteen thousand people. He was officially requested by the Lord Lieutenant to remain in the city pending the convening of an Admiralty court, so he was forced to stay.

His personal situation was a little embarrassing, however. He had no money at all, and not even any clothes except those he had been wearing when he made his escape, and those had been ruined by the seawater. The citizens offered him hospitality, and he did not hesitate to accept it from Madame Adrienne Chanoyes, a handsome blonde widow with a house of her own facing the harbor.

Smith spent a total of five weeks as Adrienne's houseguest. Although the English commercial agent at Bordeaux, a position equivalent to that of consul-general in later times, made some bald assumptions concerning their relationship in his report to London, Smith himself never hinted that their relationship was anything but platonic.

Whatever the situation, Adrienne treated Smith with the utmost kindness. Her late husband had been a sea captain and as his clothes fitted Smith she gave them to him. She went to the market every day to personally select food for the man who had been washed up on her doorstep, and she did him an even greater service. She was thoroughly familiar with French Admiralty laws, and she advised Smith that he had a legal right to share in the loot from the privateers that the French Crown had seized. With her help he entered a claim for a reasonable portion of the prize money.

The hearing was held at the end of December. The English commercial agent from Bordeaux, Charles

Bridges, was present at the proceedings, to ensure that full justice was done to a British subject. He also had the duty of making a full report of the matter, in writing, to the Privy Council in London. The hearing was over in just two days. Some of the pirates had been captured, and with nothing to lose, as they were on their way to the gallows, they confirmed the story Smith told of his capture and subsequent involuntary presence on board the *Sauvage*. Smith was awarded a share of the prize money.

The court not only absolved him and cleared his name, but extended to him the thanks of the French government for his help in recovering stolen property. In appreciation, they awarded him the sum of 3600 gold crowns, the equivalent of more than 2000 English pounds. It was a staggering sum.

Smith decided to celebrate. He traveled to Paris, taking Adrienne with him. The little holiday lasted for several days, during which Smith bought himself a whole new wardrobe, including a helmet and corselet of silver and steel, which cost more than two hundred pounds. He kept only another one hundred pounds for travel expenses, and presented the rest of the prize money to Adrienne as a gift. She in return gave him a miniature portrait of herself, which was eventually owned by one of Smith's great-great-grand-nephews.

Now suitably funded and dressed, Smith left Paris alone, embarking on the last stage of his journey to England. He traveled on to Cherbourg, which had been a sleepy medieval port but had become a center for Anglo-French trade, used by merchants from both countries for trading with the cities of western England. After a few days Smith reserved passage on a merchantman traveling to Bristol. He paid the master to drop him off at Plymouth, as he still considered that city to be his headquarters.

 **27**

THE voyage from Cherbourg to Plymouth lasted almost a week, for the weather and the Channel were rough. Smith was anxious to reach England and disappointed by this added difficulty. At least, he noted, he was one of the few people on board who did not become sick. He spent his thirty-seventh birthday trying to cross the Channel.

When he finally went ashore at Plymouth on January 12, 1616, he did not realize that he had just completed his last adventure. The rest of his life would be spent in England. He was already considered to be far advanced into middle age, living as he did when such rudimentary sanitary practices as frequent bathing were not considered healthful, and when medical science consisted largely of superstition.

Smith did not waste time thinking of his age, however. He wanted only to organize a colonizing venture to New England, that goal for which he had already suffered so much. The misfortunes of his last venture were, in his opinion, only the ordinary hazards of the trade, and he disregarded them. He was anxious to raise more funds and organize a new company so that he could return to the New World, which he considered his true home.

Although he was eager to resume his explorations, his investors, he was astonished to discover, were not so enthusiastic. To begin with, no one seemed surprised to find him still alive. News of his survival and the events at La Rochelle had preceded him to England through several sources, including the official report by Commercial Agent Bridges. Everyone who knew him had had time to recover from initial amazement.

Sir Ferdinando received Smith coolly. Smith was hurt, but Sir Ferdinando let his friendship be influenced by business. He had a strong faith in the future of English colonization in the New World, but his faith in John Smith had undergone some drastic changes. He had invested a considerable sum on Smith's ill-fated venture of 1615, and he had lost it all. He was not willing to give Smith the unqualified support he had in the past.

The Duke of Richmond also refused support. Behind the Duke, of course, stood the Duchess. For reasons of her own, one of them perhaps involving the report Bridges made to the Privy Council concerning Smith's interlude with Adrienne Chanoyes, she, too, had cooled in her enthusiasm. In any event, the ample Richmond purse was closed to Smith.

Unable to proceed along these lines, Smith returned to London, and to work, to finish the manuscript of *A Description of New England*. He remembered all the offers of financial help that had been extended to him before, and he hoped to reawaken interest and enthusiasm with his new book. Hall was still making money from Smith's first effort, and he showed no hesitation about publishing *A Description of New England*. The book was registered at Stationers' Hall on the third of June. In two weeks the printing was complete, and the book created a stir with the reading public. But the nobles and merchants were still unimpressed. The success of the book in no way compensated for Smith's failure on his last venture. Eventually *A Description of New England* would inspire the Pilgrims, who were then living in Holland, but that would be small consolation for Smith.

His financial situation was even more precarious than he liked to admit. He was barely able to pay for rent and basic living expenses from his inheritance, and he was deeply in debt to a number of creditors, all of whom were demanding immediate payment. He was forced to promise them large shares of the earnings from *A Description of New England* in order to stay out of debtors' prison and avoid complete disgrace.

It was during this unfortunate period of Smith's life that Pocahontas and her husband, John Rolfe, came to England for their great social triumph. Lord De La Warr had returned from Jamestown, and the Rolfes stayed at the De La Warr townhouse in London. Pocahontas's social success was unprecedented, and crowds dogged her every footstep, even waiting outside the De La Warr house every morning to catch a glimpse of her. Pocahontas did not seem to mind and always spoke a few words to those nearest her, but eventually her husband convinced her that she should be driven around town in a carriage; he was afraid she might inadvertently be injured. The young Indian was dressed in the latest English fashions and went sightseeing in London to prepare for a royal audience at Whitehall. It is ironic, although Pocahontas did not know it, that she was living only a short distance from the lodgings of John Smith.

Pocahontas was, in her own way, a very effective propagandist for New World colonization. Her beauty would have made her stand out anywhere, but in England she was exotic; and in 1616 Indians from the New World were fashionable, good-looking or not. Her intelligence also occasioned comment; Pocahontas had not learned to hide her natural wit as many women of the English aristocracy found it prudent to do. Her very presence excited interest in her far-off homeland.

Every door in London was opened to Mistress Rolfe, especially after her highly successful meetings with the royal family. Queen Anne was enchanted by her, finding it a miracle that a "heathen" should have become not only a Christian but a cultured one at that. She considered the young Indian woman, the daughter of a so-called savage king, to be of a rank almost equal to her own, which made it much easier for her to be friendly. Charles, Prince of Wales, certainly considered Pocahontas to be of similar social standing, and there were even a few rumors, soon laid to rest, that the Prince was in love with her. In reality, Charles regarded her as a slightly older sister and good friend, a relationship of which his mother approved. Pocahontas often attended the theater with the Queen and the Prince of Wales. Probably due to this association, Charles developed a strong interest in colonization, which he actively encouraged after he took the throne.

By the early winter of 1617 Pocahontas had brought so much attention to the efforts of the London Company that over two hundred immigrants had applied and been accepted for passage to Virginia. Such was the interest in the colony that a second ship had to be purchased to accommodate the overflow of passengers.

When Pocahontas eventually met King James, even that dour monarch unbent. He was charmed, not by her beauty but by her word-for-word knowledge of the translation of the Bible he had commissioned scholars to make, and by her liking for the uninspired food that was served at his table.

During this time of her great triumph, Captain John Smith was regarded with contempt by every London hostess. It was his own fault. When Frances would not see him, he took to living openly with one of the most notorious courtesans in the country, Barbara Courtenay. He made no attempt to be discreet but appeared in public with her.

Barbara Courtenay was a beautiful blonde who had at one time been the mistress of Prince Henry. Since his death she had been very free with her favors. As her own family had disowned her and she had no visible means of support, no gentleman would risk being seen publicly with her. And no lady would receive her socially, no matter what that lady's private morals were.

Smith was obviously defying convention by living openly with her, but it seemed he did not care. Perhaps he was upset because he could not find financial backing for his proposed new venture in colonization, but he was not powerful or wealthy enough to so completely ignore the conventions, and he suffered for it. The aristocracy, upon whose help he depended, pretended he did not exist.

Smith thus immensely complicated his already difficult problems. Even the Earl and Countess of Southampton, paying a visit to London, refused to receive him at their house, hurting not only his pride but his hopes for a future New England colony.

Smith grew increasingly desperate. Others were talking of settling in New England, even a religious sect known as the Separatists. Although exiled by King James, they had sent a representative to London to explore the possibility that they might find a permanent home on English soil in the New World. It began to seem as though Smith might be left behind in his search for financial support.

It was at this point, apparently, that Smith decided to cash in on the success of Pocahontas to serve his own ends. It was then that he wrote the footnotes concerning his alleged experience with her for *A True Relation.*

Smith's need for money was still great, and this story showed promise as a means to gain new funds. In the seventeenth century printers did not fill every page completely; they often left as much as three inches of margin at the bottom of some pages. Long footnotes could run on from one page to the next. Smith wanted to make use of these blanks, and Hall was quite willing to bring out such a printing. The revised book was published hastily.

At about this time Smith began to show a little more good sense in managing his social life. He began to appear in public occasionally without Barbara Courtenay, and a partial social thaw set in. The interest aroused by *A Description of New England* may have been in part responsible for the general warming of attitudes. No one had really been shocked by his behavior as long as he took care not to be seen with the woman.

The Earl and Countess of Southampton were the first to relent. Next was the Earl of Somerset, who had a vast palace directly opposite Smith's lodgings. Somerset was no longer as intimate with King James as he had been, and he probably felt a certain amount of sympathy for a fellow social outcast. In any event, Smith dined with him on several occasions, both ignoring their prior clash.

Although Smith's name appears nowhere in the records of people who kept careful track of the activities of Pocahontas, the story still persists that they met sometime during the year 1616. The lack of records does not necessarily mean the meeting did not take place; it simply adds a little more doubt. According to an undying tradition, the captain and the Indian saw each other at the townhouse of the De La Warrs. This is not likely, as Smith probably had no more than a passing acquaintance with them, and was not likely to have been invited to a social gathering at their house. One possible connection was Commodore Newport, who had brought Pocahontas to England and who had most likely visited Smith since his return. But this is another theory for which proof is impossible.

According to one version of the meeting, Pocahontas did not know Smith when he was presented to her. Perhaps he had changed over the years, if she had indeed met him previously. She had certainly changed, being dressed now in the latest English fashions, wearing a necklace of amethysts that Queen Anne had given her. Instead of wearing her hair loose or in braids, it was now piled high on her head in the intricate style of the times.

Smith retells the story of his first alleged meeting with Pocahontas in his *General Historie of Virginia, New England, and the Summer Isles,* published in 1624, and goes on to describe his reunion with her in the house of Lord and Lady De La Warr. He admits that at first she did not recognize him, but goes on to say that she remembered him a moment later, and was delighted that they had met again.

Almost naturally, it would seem, in the wake of John

Smith, various wilder legends grew up around the supposed London meeting. According to one, Smith and Pocahontas had been in love in Virginia. When they met again in London they realized they still loved each other but said a final farewell for the sake of propriety. This story is almost as absurd as the one that claims Smith still loved Pocahontas but she rebuffed him, and he left with a broken heart. If Smith's heart was broken it was over his lack of success in organizing a new colonizing venture, not over a mythical lost love.

If Pocahontas heard the story of her dramatic rescue of Smith from death at her father's hands, she was probably amused. By that time she was accustomed to dealing with wild rumors. Most of the major nobles of the land were whispered to be in love with her, and the belle of London had learned to take gossip with a grain of salt.

The only remaining portrait of her shows her in the stiff formal attire of the age, her long hair hidden by a hat, with a curiously wistful expression. This portrait appears in Smith's book, *The Generall Historie of Virginia, New England, and the Summer Isles*, published in 1624. Two other paintings of her were irreparably damaged on a voyage to Virginia.

 **28**

THE authenticity of Smith's Pocahontas story did not matter to most of its readers, and the new edition of *A True Relation* sold well, greatly increasing interest in the New World. As the book's popularity rose, so did Smith's. By the autumn of 1616 he had terminated his affair with Barbara Courtenay and went to visit Sir Ferdinando in Plymouth.

This time his search for financial support was more successful. Sir Ferdinando's enthusiasm for exploration had overcome his desire to add to his riches, and he was once again willing to risk backing Smith. He invested about two thousand pounds.

Others were quick to follow. The Earl of Southampton invested an even larger sum. Wealthy men from Plymouth, Bristol, and Exeter who had read *A Description of New England* also hurried to give their support. Smith suddenly found himself extremely busy outfitting a new expedition, which included buying three ships and hiring crews.

He did run into two unexpected difficulties. He had difficulty recruiting prospective colonists, a circumstance for which he had not planned. His descriptions of the New World wilderness, its hardships and its obstacles, had been too accurate and too vivid, and hard-working citizens were reluctant to risk themselves and their families in such an extreme situation. Smith was not interested in reckless adventurers of a more hardy but aggressive type and would not give them passage, but the preferred type of citizen remained wary.

The second problem was the severe weather. Later scientists have deduced that, due to a change in sunspot activity, the earth was suffering a "little ice-age" during the early part of the seventeenth century. All that Smith knew was that winter came early to England in 1616 and was the harshest the country had seen in years. In northern latitudes the glaciers were advancing, and fierce gales and sea ice kept all shipping port-bound. Some of the people who had agreed to try their luck at colonizing the new land took a look at the ice and snow piled on the decks of the three waiting ships and decided that things could only be worse in the New World. When they backed out Smith was left with even fewer colonists.

Finally, rather than wait too long, forcing his investors to wait for a return on their money, Smith decided to send all three vessels to the fishing banks in Newfoundland as soon as the weather broke in the spring. Smith's planning was long-range now. He was hoping that profits from the fishing venture would make investors eager for greater ventures, thus giving him the time he needed to look more thoroughly for the type of colonist he wanted.

The ships sailed in March 1617, without him. Smith then made a personal tour of the communities in western England whose nobles and wealthy merchants were qualified by the terms of the King's charter to invest in settlements in New England. Driven by the restless energy that was his trademark, Smith traveled as far north as Shrewsbury, visiting such cities as Hereford, Gloucester, Worcester, and Cheltenham. He spent six weeks in Bristol as the guest of Sir Edward Eames, a baronet who was one of Smith's more ardent advocates.

When the three ships returned to Plymouth in late August 1617 it was obvious their fishing trip had been successful. They had brought back a rich haul, and Smith was able to pay his investors two pounds and five shillings for each pound they had invested. His prospects were greatly improved. Sir Ferdinando called a meeting in Plymouth for those interested in Smith's ventures, and in late September a significant number of men of substance had gathered there.

Smith addressed them in the Citadel, a stone fort at the head of one of the inlets to the port, built by Henry VIII. The meeting was unofficial, but as Sir Ferdinando was Governor of Plymouth, he had the right to use the building as he wished. Smith must have used the atmosphere of the place to his advantage, speaking at his persuasive best, trying to inspire the wealthiest men of western England. He undoubtedly reminded his audience that Sir John Hawkins had used the fort as his headquarters when he was Admiral of the fort. Sir Francis Drake had slept in the same room in which Smith was speaking, before setting out in 1577 on his voyage around the world. Sir Humphrey Gilbert had also spent time there before he left on his second voyage of discovery to the New World. Smith suggested that now the nobles and merchants had their opportunity to win immortality of the same sort as that of England's greatest mariners.

His speech brought immediate results. His audience pledged large amounts of money right there, so much

213

that even Smith was astonished. When he added up the pledges he realized that there would be enough to send a fleet of twenty ships and over one thousand settlers to the New World.

Smith was given a new title, issued under the royal patent for New England. Before the audience he had so impressed, Smith was presented, with an inscribed sealed parchment by Sir Ferdinando. This testified that Smith was now Admiral of New England, a rank he would hold for the rest of his life.

Smith preferred the title of Captain. Perhaps he chose not to use Admiral because of the unfortunate outcome of this grand beginning. The investors eventually began to quarrel among themselves, and most of the wonderful pledges were not redeemed. The great plan collapsed. Smith later wrote, "Nothing but a voluntary fishing expedition was effected, for all this air." He had begun to suspect the truth even before his investors left to go back to their homes.

Smith's new plan was characteristically ambitious, but uncharacteristically complex. He hoped that the expedition could start out in 1618. He would go to New England himself, with a small band of hard-working men, to build a fort and a settlement, and to clear fields and plant grain. Eight to ten months later the other settlers would begin arriving, and by then the colony would be ready for them. Smith's potential backers seemed delighted by his ideas and fully agreed with them—before they went back to their own homes and forgot all about them. Few men produced the cash Smith needed.

Smith spent over an entire year on the project, working hard to organize it. By the end of this time, when he realized that he did not in fact have the support he needed, he knew he would have to find someone more influential than Southampton or Sir Ferdinando to head the company's directorate. He told no one of his plans, fearing to lose the support of those principal backers he had left, but he returned to London to learn the current thinking about ventures such as his. He made frequent trips to taverns visited by the wealthy to listen to gossip and survey the political climate.

The Prince of Wales, still a youth, had no power and could not help Smith, however much he might have wanted to. The most important man in the country was George Villiers, a dashing young man in his mid-twenties. Villiers occupied Somerset's old place in the King's esteem, but he was infinitely more energetic and aggressive. He had received a number of honors and was already the Earl of Buckingham. He was made a Marquess on New Year's Day of 1618, and five years later would be made a Duke. He was one of the wealthiest nobles in the land, and he was given the task of supervising the education of Prince Charles. His energies were not limited to these duties, however, and he had been given a mandate to completely reorganize the Army. He had also taken command of the Navy.

Smith first considered applying directly to Buckingham for help, but he soon realized that this would be a waste of time. Buckingham had his own personal court, and he was swamped with applicants and daily requests for special favors. Furthermore, Buckingham had shown no interest whatsoever in the New World. His preoccupation was with the balance of power in Europe, and he vigorously applied himself to diplomacy in that field. He was, in effect, the British foreign secretary, along with all his other duties, and he was involved in playing the

215

great nations of the Continent against one another.

It was obvious to Smith that he had to look elsewhere for help. He chose as his target Buckingham's tutor, Francis Bacon, one of the greatest scholars of the age. After the death of Richard Hakluyt in 1616 only Bacon had the geographer's same zeal for scientific research. Bacon, too, had the same power to authorize the use of royal monies for scientific projects. Bacon was a man in his late fifties, a very respectable age for the times. His many talents included philosopher, playwright, essayist, attorney, and statesman, as well as scientist with a scientist's typically unquenchable thirst for knowledge.

Bacon himself had experienced a great rise in power. In 1613 the King had made him Attorney General, and early in 1617, with the aid of Buckingham, he had become Lord Keeper of the Great Seal. The title was an honored one, although the position itself meant little. It was an important step toward his next promotion, when in January of 1618 he became Lord Chancellor and a member of the Privy Council. Everyone expected that he would soon be granted a position in the peerage; a few months later King James made him Baron Verulam.

It seemed obvious to Smith that Bacon was the man to whom he should apply for help. There was one unfortunate obstacle to this seemingly perfect solution: Smith had never had the opportunity to meet the great scholar. Another problem was that he needed to think of some opening to stimulate Bacon's interest in the New World. Smith came up with a unique solution.

After giving the matter considerable thought, Smith sat down to write another book. This was not to be a book for the general reading public of England, however; it was to be written for only one reader. Smith

216

worked furiously. He shut himself up in a room and had all his meals brought in so that he would not be forced to interrupt himself even to eat. Writing almost continuously, he completed the manuscript in about three months. He called the work *New England's Trials*. The whole theme of the book, and its sole purpose, was to demonstrate the feasibility and great potential in establishing colonies in that northern section of the New World.

When the book was completed, Smith arranged with George Hall to have it printed. The estimated expense of the printing was so great, however, that Smith ordered only two thousand copies for a first edition. If they sold he would then consider another printing, while the proceeds would pay for his expenses.

Smith immediately sent a copy off to Bacon, enclosing a long letter that was very difficult for him to write. He did not like humbling himself to beg for favors, but he was forced to do so by circumstances, and he bluntly admitted it in so many words. True to his nature, he decided that speaking with candor was the best policy, and he withheld nothing. The Spanish, the Dutch, and the French were so active in New World colonization, he wrote, that he was certain that if he went to them with his plans they would show an interest. He preferred not to go to them, however, if he could get help in England. "Nature," he wrote, "doth bind men to beg at home."

He made a careful list of his qualifications to lead an expedition to the New England territories, and he informed Bacon that he had nineteen years of experience in hazardous pursuits. He also added, tactfully, that he was willing to serve the scholar in any capacity, whether at home in England or abroad.

217

Smith's actual request seemed very modest, at least on the surface. He asked Bacon for a small warship from the Royal Navy. He did not want it as an outright gift, merely as a loan on detached service of some sort. Naturally it would be manned by sailors from the Royal Navy; the Admiralty would undoubtedly refuse to have it any other way. Experienced soldiers, men of good and stable character, would also be required to accompany Smith's advance party and help build a town for the settlers who would follow.

Bacon undoubtedly saw the surface modesty of Smith's request right away. King James himself would be openly committed to the project if he sent a Navy ship manned by Royal Navy sailors to start a colony that would be initially settled by Army troops. The Crown would be placing its own dignity at risk, as neither the King nor his Privy Council could possibly allow such a colony to fail. Smith asked only for the relatively small sum of five thousand pounds, pointing out that over one hundred thousand pounds had already been spent in Virginia without much to show for it. But Bacon, as Lord Chancellor, knew that once the Crown was committed, it would have to rely repeatedly on Treasury funds to ensure the success of Smith's dream of a New England colony. James was a frugal King and would not have been pleased with the prospect.

Francis Bacon, unfortunately for Smith, was too busy with his newly delegated responsibilities and the duties he had assumed to undertake a new and hazardous venture. He had too many other projects to occupy his attention. He sent a brief but courteous answer to the explorer in which he claimed that he was not in a position to act on Smith's requests.

218

Smith was bitterly disappointed but tried to take it in stride. He had dedicated his presentation copy of *New England's Trials* to Francis Bacon. When he could not obtain the help in this manner of a single powerful sponsor, he decided to aim for a broader audience. He resolved to try a little mass fund-raising.

He knew that the fishing industry had benefited greatly from the expeditions to Newfoundland, including the fishing vessels he himself had sent out. He therefore ordered some flyleafs printed, and dedicated other copies of the book to the "right worshipful, the Master, the Wardens, and the Company of the Fish-mongers." Still other copies were dedicated to various gentlemen in Devonshire and Cornwall, of whom he had hopes; others to the aldermen of Barnstaple; another to the Lord Mayor of Exeter. He worked furiously, more active than he had been for a long time. He had copies of his maps of New England printed in batches of hundreds, and gave them away to anyone he thought might be a potential investor in the enterprise he wanted so badly. But it seemed that the harder he worked, the less he accomplished.

In 1618 England fell into a financial recession. Even the Crown had to cut back its expenses. The staff of gentlemen-in-waiting at the Court was reduced, and King James requested that the Privy Council plan a new system of taxation to bring in increased revenues. Higher rates of interest were being charged by the money lenders, and private citizens in small country towns were hoarding gold. Even the very wealthy were being careful of their spending and did not feel they could afford to risk investment in a New World colony that had not yet even been started.

It is curiously ironic that the group most interested in Smith's idea was the almost impoverished Separatists, exiles who were living in Amsterdam and Leyden. The little band of religious nonconformists had read *A Description of New England* and had been fascinated by it. They obtained two copies of the work from members of their sect living underground in England. When they read *New England's Trials* they became even more firmly convinced that they should cross the Atlantic to establish a settlement of their own in New England, a place where they would be left in peace yet could live and bring up their families on English soil.

One of the leaders of the sect, and its primary propagandist, was William Brewster. He spent much of his time writing tracts that were considered seditious by the Crown, but he decided, despite the very great personal danger, to journey to England to gather more information about the New England territories.

The journey reveals the typical courage of the man who would become known as Elder Brewster, religious leader of the Pilgrim colony. He did not conform to the later grim stereotype of a Pilgrim Father, but was a robust and hearty man, even in middle age. Like Smith, he refused to shrink from danger, no matter what the circumstance. He was perfectly aware that if the authorities discovered his presence in England they would send out every bailiff in the country to look for him. If caught, he would be tried, most likely found guilty of treason, and hanged.

His friends were very careful to take every possible precaution to conceal his identity while he was in England. Brewster moved constantly, not spending more than a very few nights under the same roof, and always using an assumed name. In addition, he saw only those people whose discretion he knew he could trust. Unfortunately, this thick cloak of secrecy around his visit to England, while necessary at the time, deprived later generations of a true account of his meetings and discussions with John Smith.

As a result, the known facts are few. Sometime during 1618 a member of the Separatists communicated secretly with Smith. It is assumed, reasonably enough, that he obtained a pledge from Smith that he would not reveal Brewster's presence to the authorities. After these assurances were received, the two strong-minded men met on several occasions.

Unfortunately both their aims and their personalities clashed. Smith's goal was to establish a royal colony that would grow every year in both size and influence. In time the province would become self-supporting through shipping the sought-after resources of the New World to England. Lumber, fish, and sassafras should soon bring the settlement out of debt. Brewster had no interest in these plans. He wanted only a safe asylum for his band of Separatists, a refuge where they could worship in peace. A bustling settlement that was a New World replica of those he sought to escape in England had nothing to recommend it in his eyes.

The Separatists did not hesitate to acknowledge their debt to Smith, but they would not consider becoming citizens in a community in which they could once again be deprived of their religious freedom. They insisted on the right to set up their own colony, and they planned to elect a governor and council from among themselves, rather than have one appointed by the Crown or by representatives of the Crown.

Although they did not agree with Smith's ideas, the Separatists respected him, and they needed the advantage of his experience in living in the New World. Above all, they respected his ability to understand and get along with the Indians. They knew that he was the man who had succeeded in putting Jamestown on a functioning basis. Out of all Smith's countrymen, it was this splinter group that most fully appreciated what he had accomplished in the New World.

As a result, Brewster offered him leadership of the military aspect of the Separatist colony. He would have full control over the defenses and armaments of the settlement, and everyone would be responsible to him in these matters. He, in return, would be responsible to the governor and the council. It is not known whether or not Brewster gave any thought to the almost inevitable conflict that would have occurred had Smith accepted this proposal, for Smith's temperment was very different from that of the settlement the Separatists wanted.

Although Smith found the terms disagreeable, he was nonetheless tempted by the offer. He was so desperate to return to the New World, which had occupied his dreams for so long, that he considered giving up his own ambitious plans to go with a small band of poverty-stricken religious malcontents to New England. He continued his negotiations with Brewster sporadically, with each of them presenting terms and rejecting counterdemands until sometime in 1619.

Eventually Smith broke off negotiations. The Separatists were too inflexible for him, and they ultimately refused any compromise or any basis for an agreement other than their own. However annoyed Smith may have been, he was still a man of honor and did not turn

Brewster over to the authorities.

It was only this conflict of wills and ideals that kept Smith from becoming a member of the first lasting colony in New England. Unable to come to terms with Smith, the Separatists hired for their military leader a former Army officer, Captain Miles Standish. Eventually, after overcoming many obstacles, they crossed the Atlantic and landed in New England in 1620 at the place Smith had named New Plymouth. There they were met by Smith's old friend Squanto.

During the following years Smith never forgot the Separatists, and harbored a continuing grudge against them. He felt they had taken unfair advantage of his knowledge and experience, using him as best they could but refusing to hire him as their leader. On several occasions he made fun of them for their frugality, their "singularity," and their "contempt for authority," by which he no doubt meant the common forms of authority in England, as they had a very great regard for their own strict discipline.

Even while Smith negotiated with Brewster, he continued with his other efforts to raise funds for the enterprise he wanted to lead. Nothing came of it. As he wrote later, "All availed no more than to hew rocks with oyster shells."

Smith had no desire to return to Virginia. The early days of that colony were over, and the tobacco plantations were now well established, bringing investors a good return on their money. New England was his real love, and he thought continually of its great wilderness, which appealed to him far more than Virginia had. He was obsessed with New England. He wrote, traveled, talked, and otherwise incessantly badgered every man of

223

wealth in England who might be a potential backer.

Not much is known of Smith's activities from 1618 to 1622. As Admiral of New England he had neither sailors nor ships, and as self-elected governor of a royal colony he had neither colonists nor settlement, and no arms or provisions. It would seem that he continued to live in London, but he had few friends and little social life. He was so totally obsessed with his cause that he had no time left for any other activities.

In 1621, still pursuing his dream, he brought out another, small edition of *New England's Trials*. He had been spending his own money freely in his efforts to raise more funds, and his finances were beginning to suffer. In 1622, not knowing what else to do, he published a public edition of *New England's Trials*. Its sale enabled him to live comfortably once again.

Toward the end of this period Smith began to understand that he must abandon the dream of personally leading an expedition to New England. He was now forty-two years old, handicapped by chronic illnesses for the first time in his life. He developed a dry cough that persisted to the end of his life, and an ache in his bones bothered him continually. No single event forced him to realize that his dream was ended; it was rather that circumstances had combined against him in a long, slow process of erosion.

Despite himself, he had to face the facts. However enthusiastic he might be on the subject of colonization, no investors were yet willing to risk large sums of money in that field.

Other nations had recognized the gains to be made from colonization, and the Dutch, French, and Spanish were engaged in a desperate race for territory and influence. The British were awakening very slowly to the benefits of an expansionist policy. This slowness was frustrating to Smith, an early pioneer who had spent over fifteen years trying to make his countrymen aware of the trend.

Although he had given up hopes of returning to the New World, he would not entirely give up the struggle on behalf of colonization. He knew that his own days of adventure were ended, but he believed it was his duty to continue trying to alert the English people. Naturally his motives were not completely unselfish. Knowing that his contributions had not been properly appreciated, and with his vanity unappeased, he wanted the recognition from England that he was accorded by France, Holland, and the German states.

He was angered by the fate of Henry Hudson, his friend, who had been unknown and unappreciated during his life. Left by a mutinous crew to die of cold and starvation on the shores of the bay that now bore his name, he was only now, after his untimely death, being hailed as a great patriot and hero.

Although Smith had been determined not to meet a similar end, he was caught in a cruel and unavoidable trap. Forces outside his control had prevented him from returning to New England to set up the colony that he knew would succeed and win lasting fame for its leaders. He was afraid that their efforts would dwarf his own accomplishments, and that in later ages he would be relatively forgotten.

He had been obsessed with the New World for most of his adult life, yet his name was not synonymous with

Jamestown, and no one thought of him as a Raleigh or as a Henry Hudson. His strength was failing, and he wanted a means to achieve a double purpose: to aid the cause of British colonization, and to win for himself a permanent place in English history.

 **29**

F<small>INALLY</small>, in the winter of 1621–22, Smith's life became more orderly, quieter, and a little more realistically-oriented. During this same period he and the Duchess of Richmond became reconciled once again. She, too, was growing older and was tired of having to maintain a continuing social facade. She was saddened by the chronic illness of her husband, who was to receive a duchy in 1623 only to die a year later.

When she and Smith resumed their friendship it was on a deeper basis than it had been previously. Neither had known many real, lifelong friends, and they were happy to find that their relationship had survived separation. They were both badly in need of a friend.

The Duchess was a good influence on Smith. He confided in her. She in return was able to supply a certain degree of common sense to his outlook that, despite all his shrewdness, he had always lacked. She convinced him to put a final end to his dream of returning to New England to establish a colony.

Instead, and probably under her influence, Smith decided to devote himself completely to a new and for him more reasonable project. In the spring of 1621 he had conceived the idea of writing a complete history of the

New World to his present day. In the beginning he had envisaged it as another propaganda project, albeit larger and more complex than the others. He had sought the support of various patrons in the nobility for what he hoped would eventually win him support for the colony he wanted to build. Now he enlarged his horizons even further, deciding to write a comprehensive work to be the definitive masterwork on the subject of English colonization in the New World.

He spent more than three years on the project, under the patient encouragement of Frances. He called the result *The Generall Historie of Virginia, New England and the Summer Isles.* He worked more carefully than he ever had before, spending months in research. Afraid that he would not win recognition as a great colonizer, he was determined to be remembered as a great historian. Naturally he made sure that his own achievements were not slighted.

He wrote most of the book in his own lodgings, but during the final weeks of the illness of Ludovic, Frances's husband, he moved into the Richmond palace. His sole purpose in doing so was to offer comfort to the dying man and to Frances, who had been his friend for so many years. Naturally, some members of the nobility took a dim view of the move, but that their interpretation of the relationship was false is indicated by the furious denial Frances made. She would not have lashed out so indignantly at her critics had her friendship with Smith at that time been other than platonic. It would have been totally against convention to have him living in the same palace with her and her husband had this not been the case.

The Generall Historie was completed in the early sum-

228

mer of 1624 and was registered for publication on July 12 of the same year. Although George Hall had died, his sons had inherited his business, and they published the book. By ironic coincidence it was published only a few days after the complete financial collapse of the London Virginia Company. The disaster was caused in a large part by the continued shortsighted insistence of the directors, who diverted energies of the colony into fruitless searches for diamonds and gold. Nothing could disabuse them of this dream, and they continued to demand that the colonists spend most of their time hunting precious metals, until they went bankrupt. The scandal of the Company's failure ignited interest in Smith's book, and practically guaranteed a large sale.

The book was filled with maps. Smith had redrawn his maps of Virginia, the Chesapeake Bay, and New England, and he had refined them. He also included one based on originals drawn by other men, showing the Summer Isles, now known as Bermuda. It contained the engraving by Simon van der Paas drawn from the pen-and-ink sketch Smith had made of himself. The first edition was dedicated to Frances, Duchess of Richmond, in recognition of their long friendship.

The Generall Historie consisted of much material that Smith had published previously, and altogether it made up six volumes. The first volume was a history of the efforts to colonize Virginia before 1605. In it Smith paid tribute to Sir Walter Raleigh. It was a courageous thing to do, for Raleigh's final expedition to the Caribbean in 1617 had been a failure, and he had been executed by order of the Crown the following year. Smith's tribute could thus be construed as an indirect reproach to King James. Although most of England shared Smith's sentiments, it took a very brave man to set them down in print.

The second and third volumes were revised versions of Smith's previously published work on the establishment of the Jamestown colony. He seized the chance to give a prominent place to Pocahontas. He not only retold the story of his meeting with her and elaborated on it, but made frequent other references to her interlaced with accounts of his journeys into the interior of Virginia. This book, more than the footnoted version of *A True Relation*, is responsible for the undying popularity of the John Smith–Pocahontas legend.

The fourth volume was the story of the Virginia colony from the time Smith left until the early months of 1624. He was quite clear in laying blame on the greedy investors for the problems the colony had suffered, but his enthusiasm for the settlement itself, and for its future, was not dimmed.

The fifth volume was the history of the discovery, settlement, and subsequent development of the Summer Isles. The first known discoverer of the islands had been a Spaniard, Juan de Bermúdez, in the sixteenth century, who had been carrying a cargo of hogs to Cuba. Some of the animals had escaped, with the result that Great Bermuda, or Main Island, was now supplied with a large number of wild pigs, a happy addition to native food sources. George Somers, on his way to Jamestown in 1609, had been shipwrecked there, and the British had given the islands his name, which had been corrupted in popular usage to the Summer Isles.

In 1612 the Virginia Company had taken possession of the Bermudas, establishing a small colony under the leadership of Henry More. Smith's history of this settlement was inaccurate, but it was through no fault of his own. He had no firsthand knowledge of the situation and had been forced to rely on information given him by the Virginia Company. This material had been misleading, but Smith had accepted it in good faith.

The sixth and final volume was Smith's history of New England. In part it was a revised version of *A Description of New England,* combined with a collection of essays recently written by others who had visited the New World. Smith could not refrain from writing open propaganda, using abundant superlatives to describe the land and the future he knew it would enjoy. His constant theme was that English citizens of every class should emigrate to New England.

The Generall Historie can be regarded as Smith's best book. Although he only feigns modesty in the description of his exploits and accomplishments, the book is basically dignified and witty, as befits a long labor of love. It is, in the main, a tribute to Smith himself.

Smith personally paid for publication of the exceptionally large first printing—seven thousand copies—which strained his resources. The book was an immediate success, however, and all copies sold out within two years. A second large printing was brought out in 1626 and sold even more rapidly. A third printing was published the next year. The book remained popular. Two editions were even brought out after Smith's death, one in 1632 and another in 1635.

The Generall Historie eventually made a good profit, but Smith did not enjoy much of it; the primary beneficiaries were his sister and brother. Such a large, many-volumed book was expensive to publish, especially in large quantities, and Smith's standard of living suffered as a result.

231

The more successful the book, the larger the sums Smith was forced to pay the printers.

He consequently had to give up one of the rooms in his suite, buy less expensive clothes, and eat more modest meals at less elegant taverns. Smith did not complain, perhaps because he was at last enjoying a certain sense of fulfillment. He knew that due to his efforts England was finally awakening to the great possibilities inherent in the colonization of New England. In a way he was achieving his dream.

Smith practically ignored the Separatists in his volume on New England. Nonetheless, he continued to follow the establishment and development of their colony with great interest. At last, in 1629, Smith believed that his propagandizing had borne real fruit. He wrote, "Now this year a great company of good rank, zeal, means, and quality have made a great stock, and with six good ships in the months of April and May, they set sail from the Thames to the Bay of Massachusetts, otherwise called Charles River." He was convinced that his own work had resulted in establishment of the Massachusetts Bay Colony by the Puritans, and that the city of Boston was an outgrowth of his efforts.

With the publication of *The Generall Historie* Smith gained at last the social standing he had sought. He was no longer regarded as a fading celebrity, a one-time explorer; he was able to rank among the intellectuals of London. He was considered an authority on the New World, and was treated as the equal of other famous men.

His life as an author completely absorbed him. In 1626 he wrote a short and very unusual book. Friends had expressed curiosity about life at sea, and had been fascinated with the stories Smith had to tell. From his time spent aboard ships he had learned of the daily life of sailors. One of Smith's friends, Sir Samuel Saltonstall, thought it would be a good idea for Smith to write a handbook for young men who wanted to go to sea to seek their fortunes.

The resulting book bore the strange title *An Accidence; or, the Pathway to Experience*. The book really was a volume of advice to young adventure-seekers. Because more and more young Englishmen were interested in careers at sea, it proved the most successful of all of Smith's books. It was first printed in 1626. The next year a new edition was printed, under a different and more explicit title: *The Seaman's Grammar.*

The book sold equally well under both titles, thus earning a place as one of the curiosities in the history of publishing. New editions under the name of *An Accidence* were published in 1627 and 1636. *The Seaman's Grammar* had an even longer life, and expanded versions written by others were published in 1653, 1691, and 1692.

Smith, along with his friends and most of his contemporaries, believed that the book was the first ever written on the nautical profession. As such, Smith was very proud of it. Actually, other books on the same subject had appeared at the end of the preceding century but had remained virtually unknown, even to scholars. Smith's claim was thus essentially accurate.

He was the first not only to describe life at sea but to instruct young men in matters such as navigation, gunnery, handling a ship in a storm, and the fine and necessary art of eluding pirate vessels. He also discussed such practical matters as the wardrobe a sailor needed and the type of food advisable to carry to relieve the monotony of a shipboard diet. A small book written thirty years earlier by John Davys, *The Seaman's Secrets,* discussed some of these matters, and Smith must have been aware of it, although it dealt with only a small portion of the subjects Smith covered.

Unfortunately, Smith offset much of the prestige he had gained as an author after giving up his plans to lead an expedition to New England by his poor choice of feminine companions. He and the Duchess of Richmond drifted apart, although they remained friendly. Frances grew tired of court intrigues and retired to the country to enjoy a quiet life, spending her time on Richmond estates far from London.

Smith was left at loose ends and seemed unable to learn from past experience. An ever-changing parade of mistresses made its way through his London lodgings, all of them young, blonde, and completely unacceptable socially. Smith was a little more careful than he had been with Barbara Courtenay, however. He did not insist on taking them with him when he dined at friends' houses, thus avoiding serious harm to his reputation. He was not invited to Whitehall or into the highest social circles, but he was acknowledged as an authority on the New World even if the universities refused to recognize him.

All things considered, Smith was doing well and was comfortable with himself. He was responsible for a sudden change for the worse in his status. As might be expected, it was caused by his inability to resist the flamboyant.

During the 1620s he had become acquainted with the Reverend Samuel Purchas, one of the more curious figures of that fascinating time. The short, slender clergyman was consumed with the single ambition to succeed the late Archdeacon Hakluyt as the moving force

234

and spiritual leader of his nation's discoverers and explorers. He was truly interested in new, distant, and little-known places, but he lacked the discernment and scientific background with which Hakluyt had been endowed. He wrote many books, but they contained much misleading information, primarily because he was himself unable to distinguish between the factual and the fictitious.

Purchas wanted to meet everyone in England who had traveled extensively, and he thus naturally became acquainted with Smith. Their relationship was only casual, however, as they saw each other infrequently. Although Purchas was the rector of St. Martin's Church in London, he did not much concern himself with the duties of his position. He was known primarily for the two books he published on the subject of exploration, one in 1616, the other in 1619.

In 1620 he was planning a new edition, to be called *Pilgrimes*. In either 1623 or 1624 he read a copy of a book written in Italian by Francisco Farnese, who had been the personal secretary of Sigismund Bathory, Smith's commander-in-chief in the war against the Turks. Farnese had dealt at length with Smith's exploits in that campaign. Purchas was impressed enough to translate several of these passages into English, verbatim, for his own book.

This edition of *Pilgrimes* appeared in 1625. Some of Smith's friends had known nothing of his early career in Central Europe and were surprised to learn of his exploits there. If they were inclined to consider some of the more fantastic adventures to be farfetched distortions of the truth, they did not blame Smith for them. The stories had been written by Farnese and translated by Purchas, so Smith was not considered responsible. Purchas died in a debtors' prison in 1626, thoroughly discredited.

That did not end the interest in Smith's early life, now that curiosities had been sparked by Purchas's book. Occasionally someone would ask Smith about his life as a mercenary in Europe, and the repeated inquiries gave him the idea that there might be a demand for a book on the subject. Accordingly, he began work in 1628 on *The True Travels, Adventures and Observations of Captaine John Smith*, an autobiographical account of his years before the Jamestown expedition. The very last section of the book was a series of essays of varying lengths dealing with his views on almost everything up to the time of the book's completion.

Smith registered the *True Travels* on August 29, 1629. He acted as his own publisher, but unfortunately did not have enough funds to cover his costs. He did not acquire enough capital until the following year. The book appeared in two volumes, and Smith dedicated it to the Earl of Lindsey, Lord Chamberlain of England. The Earl had been his boyhood friend, Lord Willoughby.

The basic facts of Smith's book are truthful, but he was unable to resist embroidering them, trying to make what was already an exciting story even more romantic. He repeatedly enlarges incidents even beyond the accounts given by Farnese. Consequently, scholars both in Smith's time and later have been unable and unwilling to accept much of what he relates.

Even though the core of the *True Travels* was accurate, Smith's reputation as a historian was destroyed. Not only were serious scholars unable to accept many of his stories, they were irritated by his outrageous purple prose, quite different from the more sober style he had

236

employed in previous books. Even the bare truth of his adventures would have been hard enough to believe; the exaggerations were incredible.

True Travels was a financial success, but Smith was laughed at behind his back, often by influential men who had considered him an authority on New World explorations. Smith challenged a few of his tormentors to duels, but they refused to accept the challenges. In some instances he was actually snubbed, which hurt his vanity as much, or more, than the teasing. It is possible that by then Smith really believed the truth of every word he had written, and that he was no longer able to distinguish fact from fantasy. His conduct indicates that he believed he had written an accurate autobiography.

A few friends did stand by him during these trying times, among them Sir Samuel Saltonstall. The Earl of Lindsey wrote him a gracious note of appreciation, on the surface at least accepting *True Travels* as a factual account.

All the same, it was the beginning of the end for Smith. He was upset by the attitude of the English toward him, his health was failing, and he was once again in low spirits. He was glad to accept the invitation of Sir Humphrey Mildmay, a former colonel of a royal household regiment, to spend some months at the Mildmay estate in Essex.

It was there, in the autumn of 1630, that he wrote his last book, *Advertisements for the Unexperienced Planters of New England.* It was a handbook of advice for people interested in settling in the New World, and was similar to *An Accidence* in format. It was published the following spring, and was the least successful of all of Smith's books. It contained little that had not appeared elsewhere in his writings and was basically a rehashing of old material.

Smith was preoccupied with the state of his health, and there were several veiled references to his impending death in the book. Perhaps for this reason he dedicated *Advertisements* to the Archbishop of Canterbury, whom he had not met.

He also took the opportunity to return to one of his favorite themes, the ignorance of the Jamestown investors, which had done so much harm to the colony. He could never forget his grievances against them, nor against the Separatists, whom he considered incapable of establishing a successful colony in New England. He stubbornly refused to admit that the Separatist colony at Plymouth was now thriving, after a difficult period. He also seized the chance to make fun, once again, of old enemies like Gabriel Archer, devoting much space to ridiculing their lack of abilities in the wilderness.

Advertisements also contained several poems. Although Smith had included occasional verses in previous books, these were undistinguished efforts, amounting to nothing more than little jingles.

He had not lost his faith in the New World and expressed again his total confidence in the futures of the British colonies there, urging his countrymen to migrate to the new settlements, to "this glorious land, which will prosper more than any other Country I have Known."

In the beginning of 1631 Smith left Essex to return to his London lodgings. It seemed as if his health had improved, and he began to make plans for another book to be a companion to his *Generall Historie*. This was to be called *History of the Sea* and was to be equally broad in scope. He still remembered his childhood adulation of

Drake and Hawkins, and he indicated in his notes that he wanted to dedicate this new book to their memories.

The book was to have been a complete history of every voyage of discovery made by both Englishmen and Europeans. Although it was fairly easy for Smith to find material pertaining to the Cabots and other explorers sailing under the English flag, it was much more difficult to obtain information on sailors from other lands. He became acquainted with the Dutch and Spanish ambassadors in England, paying them several visits, and he began to correspond with men in Amsterdam, Lisbon, and Paris.

It is very possible that *History of the Sea* would have become the major classic that Smith planned it to be, had he lived. His enthusiasm remained high, but it far overreached his physical strength. In May 1631 he began to have trouble breathing, so much so that he was forced to cease work on the book and take to his bed.

Smith's current mistress was his only nurse, and she was bored by his sickness and frequently left him to go out and amuse herself in the city. Smith's resources were still limited; although his books brought him a modest income, he still had not earned back his investment in them. He spent a large part of his available funds on doctors, of whom he bitterly complained, saying that they did nothing to alleviate his troubles. Very few of his friends visited him. When he knew he would live only a short time longer, Smith called in an attorney and wrote his will.

Smith named Sir Samuel Saltonstall as his executor. Most of his money and personal papers were left to friends. The Saltonstall family, as a result of its friendship with Smith, became strongly influenced by his enthusiasm for the New World. Sir Samuel's descendants eventually emigrated to Massachussetts Bay, where they became prominent leaders.

Smith left his property in Lincolnshire and all his literary rights to his sister and brother and their children. His personal souvenirs from his travels—Turkish scimitars and Indian knives, the things he considered precious—were to be given to the small handful of his loyal friends.

The Duchess of Richmond at last came to see him one day in June. Although she had arrived in London a few weeks earlier, she had just learned of his illness. The meeting was so painful, both to Smith and to the Duchess, that she remained for only a brief time. She promised to return again in a few days, but she was not to see him alive again.

Smith signed his will in the presence of his attorney, Sir Samuel, and three other witnesses on the morning of June 21, 1631. He was exhausted, and when he expressed a desire to sleep, his friends left him. When his mistress returned from the city later in the day, she found that he had died in his sleep. He was fifty-one years old.

Included among the few people who attended his funeral at the Church of St. Sepulchre were the Earl of Lindsey, Sir Samuel, and the Duchess of Bedford. Smith was buried beneath the choir vault of the church, with a modest monument over his tomb bearing the coat of arms he had won, his proof that he was a gentleman. Thirty-five years later the entire church was destroyed in London's Great Fire. Only the books and the legend of John Smith remained.

BIBLIOGRAPHY

ARBER, EDWARD, *Captain John Smith, a Critical Survey,* Birmingham, 1886.

BOYD, E., *The Story of Pocahontas and Captain John Smith,* London, 1905.

BRADLEY, A.G., *Captain John Smith,* London, 1905

BRETON, NICHOLAS, *The Courtier and the Countryman,* London, 1618.

BROWN, ALEXANDER, *The Genesis of the United States,* Boston, 1890.

BROWN, JOHN CARTER, *New England's Trials,* London, 1867.

CAMPBELL, MILDRED, *The English Yeoman Under Elizabeth and the Early Stuarts,* New Haven, 1942.

CHATTERTON, E. KEMBLE, *John Smith,* London, 1927.

COATES, MARY, *Social Life in Stuart England,* London, 1924.

CUMMING, W.P., SKELTON, R.A., & QUINN, D.B., *The Discovery of North America,* New York, 1972.

DAVIES, G., *The Early Stuarts, 1603–1660,* London, 1937.

DEANE, CHARLES, *Notes on Wingfield's Discourse on America,* Boston, 1859.

DOLE, CHRISTINA, *The English Housewife in the Seventeenth Century,* London, 1953.

DOYLE, J.A., *English in America,* London, 1882.

DRUMMOND, J.C., and Wilbraham, Anne, *The Englishman's Food,* London, 1940.

DYER, FREDERICK R., *The Pocahontas Myth,* Boston, 1901.

FISKE, JOHN, *Old Virginia and Her Neighbors,* New York, 1897.

Forerunners and Competitors of the Pilgrims and Puritans, ed. by

Charles Herbert Livermore, New York, 1912.

FULLER, THOMAS, *Worthies of England,* ed. by John Freeman, London, 1952.

GREEN, JOHN RICHARD, *A Short History of the English People,* London, 1915.

HART, ALBERT BUSHNELL, "American Historical Liars," *Harper's Magazine,* Arpil, 1915.

HAYDON, A.L., *Captain John Smith,* London, 1907.

HEYDIN, PETER, *Examen Historical, or a Discovery and Examination of the Mistakes, Falsities, and Defects in Some Modern Histories,* London, 1659.

HILLARD, GEORGE S., *The Life and Adventures of Captain John Smith,* Boston, 1834.

JOHNSON, ROSSITER, *Captain John Smith,* London, 1915.

LA FARGE, OLIVER, *A Pictorial History of the American Indian,* New York, 1956.

LEWIS, PAUL, *The Great Rogue,* New York, 1966.

NEILL, EDWARD DUFFIELD, *English Colonization of America,* London, 1871.

————, *Virginia Company in London,* London, 1869.

PALFREY, J. G., *History of New England,* Boston, 1858.

PEACHAM, HENRY, *The Compleat Gentleman,* London, 1622.

PHILLIPS, LEON, *The First Lady of America, Pocahontas,* Richmond, 1973.

PIRENNE, HENRI, *A History of Europe,* New York, 1938.

POINDEXTER, JOHN, *Captain John Smith and His Critics,* London, 1893.

PURCHAS, SAMUEL, *Haklyutus Posthumus or Purchas and His Pilgrimes, contayning a History of the World in Sea Voyages and Lande Travells, by Englishmen and Others,* London, 1625.

ROBERTS, E.P., *The Adventures of Captain John Smith,* London, 1902.

SCONES, W. BAPTISTE, *Four Centuries of English Letters,* London, 1880.

SMITH, BRADFORD, *Captain John Smith,* Philadelphia, 1953.

SMITH, JOHN, *A True Relation of such occurrences and accidents of noat as hath hapned in Virginia Since the First Planting of That Collony,* London, 1608.

242

————, *A Map of Virginia, with a Description of the Countrey,* Oxford, 1612.

————, *A Description of New England,* London, 1616.

————, *New England's Trials,* London, 1618–22.

————, *The Generall Historie of Virginia, New England and the Summer Isles,* London, 1624.

————, *An Accidence; or, the Pathway to Experience,* London, 1626.

————, *The True Travels, Adventures, and Observations of Captaine John Smith,* London, 1630.

————, *Advertisements for the Unexperienced Planters of New England,* London, 1631.

SPENCER, ROBERT F., and JENNINGS, JESSE D., et al., *The Native Americans,* New York, 1965.

SZERB, ANTHONY, "Captain John Smith in Transylvania," *Hungarian Quarterly,* VI, 1940.

TYLER, COIT, *History of American Literature,* London, 1879.

VAUGHAN, ALDEN T., *New England Frontier,* Boston, 1965.

VOGEL, VIRGIL J., *American Indian Medicine,* Norman, 1970.

WARNER, CHARLES DUDLEY, *Study of the Life and Writings of John Smith,* New York, 1881.

WHARTON, HENRY, *The Life of John Smith* (translated from the Latin with an essay by Laura Polanyi Striker), Chapel Hill, N.C., 1957.

WOODS, K.P., *The True Story of Captain John Smith,* London, 1901.

WYLER, EDITH EMERSON, *Facts Relating to the Turkish Captivity of Captain John Smith,* London, 1913.

INDEX

249